SONSHIFT

EVERYTHING CHANGES IN THE FATHER'S EMBRACE

Mel Wild

Contact information for Mel Wild: email: mwild5658@gmail.com; website: http://www.melwild.com.

Cover design: Michael Di Frisco

ISBN: 978-1517167226

DEDICATION

This book is dedicated to my sons—Brandon, Andrew, and Jason. Thank you for your faithful questioning of my assumptions which made me take a fresh look at what I believed, and for the loving relationships that helped me begin to understand the great love a father has for a son. I am so proud of you and love you with all my heart.

ACKNOWLEDGEMENTS

The pioneers, trailblazers, and fathers of the faith, both contemporary and past, some who I've mentioned by name in this book. You have taken the arrows of opposition in order to establish the "new normal" for the Christian faith in your generation, faithfully laying a foundation from which we can bravely walk off our own maps into God's advancing Kingdom.

My church family at Cornerstone who I've had the awesome privilege of leading for the last ten years. Thank you for hanging in there with me as we have explored new vistas of faith together. You're amazing! I love you all.

The blogging community at WordPress. Your constant encouragement has blessed me more than you know.

Mary Jane Kaufman, for saving me from my grammatical challenges! Your diligent work on this book was invaluable to me. I'm sure those who read it will thank you, too!

Christi Smelzer, for letting me use your cabin that helped get me started on this book after months of procrastination, and Deb Anderson for letting me use your cabin to get away and finish it. You both showed thoughtfulness and generosity that knows no bounds.

Brandon, for offering your academic expertise and helping me bring clarity to some of my thoughts. What a blessing it is for me to have such a scary brilliant son.

Finally, and most importantly, I could not possibly overstate the fact that this book would have never happened without the encouragement, inspiration and love of my best friend and beautiful bride of 35 years, Maureen. Your heart and soul is as much in this book as mine. You have shown me, over and over again, what *Sonshift* in relationship looks like by demonstrating it every day with your unshakable love and grace for me. I love you so much and so enjoy our journey together in our heavenly Father's embrace.

ENDORSEMENTS

It has been said that when you read a book, you are holding the author's life in your hands. Mel Wild's *Sonshift* is particularly fitting to that truth. You are privileged to hold and welcomed to explore Mel's life for a journey, shift by shift, by shift, deeply into a revelation that genuinely ends with the subtitle: *Everything Changes in the Father's Embrace.*

Brace yourself for challenges to your assumptions. Mel bravely leads you toward one of my favorite quotes from this book, "It's puzzling to me that we spend so much time pounding information about God into people's heads and so little time teaching them how to open their hearts to Him." He goes after the heart with unflinching passion and undeniable personal experience in order to take you straight to God's Arms. Shift by shift you will know what you cannot UN-know as you read these pages.

I love how Mel generously quotes friends, authors, leaders, speakers, prophets, teachers, and ... even me! While he unpacks his own life he also demonstrates a love for inspiration from multiple other lives. This is the kind of book I NEED as a pastor because it takes me into the humble path of authentic vulnerability coupled with valid voices from a wide spectrum of revelation. Late in *Sonshift* Mel muses, "You ARE where heaven touches earth" because he was "shifted" by the beauty of God's apostolic gift in Bill Johnson.

Get ready for everything to change, everything to shift, everything in YOU to move toward a brand new YOU because this precious pastor has had the courage to invite you into his life and book. Welcome, perhaps for the 1000th time, to the supernatural community of heaven on earth!

Bishop Randy Dean
Author of *Radiance*
Pastor, Living Word Chapel
Forest, WI

I honestly believe *Sonshift* should be required reading for all Christians. This understanding is that important. While I knew much of what Mel explains in *Sonshift* from discussions we've had over the years, he put it in a clearer, better fitting package than I already held it in. The thoughts flowed so seamlessly together that the whole picture was much more complete and vivid for me. And this book gave me some new concepts that filled in cracks in my understanding.

It's a shame how many believers experience a dysfunctional relationship with their heavenly Father, and yet quote chapter and verse to prove why they should continue that way. They're deprived of the real thing, which is so real it's unreal! Thanks for helping us all get more functional with Daddy God.

John Cummuta
Best-selling personal finance/small business author

Once in a while you will come across a book that brings a "shift" in your thinking and perspective of the world and the nature of reality. When that happens things begin to fall into place and a new world with infinite possibilities opens before you. Life begins to make more sense. As I read Mel Wild's book, *Sonshift: Everything Changes in the Father's Embrace*, I knew I had found such a book.

Mel introduces us to the true nature of Biblical faith..."intimacy in action!" There are two questions that each of us has to answer. The first is, "If there is a God, what is He really like?" and the second is, "Who am I and what does God think of me?" The quality and nature of the life we experience depends on how we answer these two questions.

Mel has managed to engage the reader in the discovery of just who our Heavenly Father is and what His character and nature are truly like. And having discovered just how good He is, we are able to discover our true identity, purpose and destiny. God is truly better than we think, so we must change the way we think about Him and ourselves. And His thoughts and intentions toward us are scandalously good! We are indeed God's most loved sons and daughters! We must learn to live as the objects of the Father's infinite affection.

I am so pleased to recommend this book to all who desire to pursue a journey in search of intimacy with the Father and discovery of their true identity and wholeness in themselves.

Dan Notley
DTN Ministries

Sonshift...a must read if you are being led by Holy Spirit into becoming a mature son of God. This book gives revelation not only of who we are - our identity, but also who our Father is and His true identity. Mel also opens the door of "grace" to new understanding...releasing Father's sons to new realms of freedom and experiences. I was greatly blessed by *Sonshift*.

Barry Thompson
Kingdom in Action Ministries

If you are thinking about reading this book then I bet you are on a journey. Likely you have discovered this gem maybe even by accident but, let me tell you, it is no accident. If you are looking for answers to the burning questions in your heart you have found the right place.

Be prepared however for something that might be unexpected. Let me explain what I mean. There are so many books out there to choose from and you have picked up this one. Most of the books we read are informative. They are filled with data that gets added to the processing unit between our ears. Some books bring us into a greater story where we experience something. Maybe it is a much needed emotional escape and refreshing. It is rare however to find a book that transforms you. These books leave a lasting impression that changes the way we think and believe. Way more than data or emotions, these rare transformative works of art get under our skin and into our souls and touch our spirits.

You may have stumbled over *Sonshift* in a very innocent way but you should be prepared to be transformed by the pages that lie ahead. So grab your favorite blanket, make a nice fire and a cup of tea then dive right in. Maybe you should bring a tissue or two just in case. Now you are ready. Before you even realize it you will be encountering your Abba in a way you didn't think was possible.

Lance Floyd
Pastor, Grace Point Church
Ridgecrest, CA

We cannot think the way we did twenty years ago. Jesus' words still ring true today, "Repent (change the way you are thinking), for the Kingdom of Heaven is here". As Mel relates his journey into an increasing fullness of this Kingdom, a journey that many of us have been experiencing today, it gives us greater hope for the future.

As I read Mel's words, my heart sings, "I am not alone in this journey." His words are simple yet profound, accurate, honest and applicable.

Rod Marquette
Senior Pastor, Destiny Church
Rochester, MN

TABLE OF CONTENTS

FOREWORD

Iconoclast: Anybody want to be one? Or maybe you already are one. If not, I predict that you're about to be one. So what is it?

The dictionary defines an iconoclast as a person who attacks cherished beliefs or institutions. This moniker fits Mel well. But even though he rather enjoys the opportunities to poke at traditions, he's also a lover of the Presence, a worshiper, he's fresh, fun, has a sheepish grin when he laughs and feels no need to be normal… just the right type to explore beyond the well-known world of conformity and orthodoxy.

Shift happens…it always has. One would have to be naive to not see that another major shift is currently impacting the body of Christ. Most believers are experiencing radical changes in their churches and in their thinking. A valiant struggle follows to try to define just what is happening.

A few brave pioneers are even daring to enter the blogosphere arena and present their newly discovered treasures for all to see… while worthy commenters look over their shoulders, encouraging and holding them accountable. The ensuing banter and rebuttals are helping to ferret out a solid Scriptural base in hopes that these truths can be installed as irrefutable doctrine in our theological hard drive.

For several years Mel has been such a risk taker. In his blog "In My Father's House" (http://melwild.wordpress.com), he has explored most of the topics presented in *Sonshift*. He has persistently mined fresh gold from stale traditions. Some of those traditions suffered a devastating toll from his mining techniques. But his prolific discoveries have opened up fresh new vistas... attracting both the curious and the scholar.

Although these truths are substantive, I enjoy knowing that Mel doesn't regard his findings as necessarily being in their final form; they are still in flux. Give this rich ore 5-10 years of rigorous crucible testing and "cross"-examination... and many of these golden discoveries will become our proven foundations for believing. Then, our new-found freedoms will make us grateful to all the brave pioneers who dared to explore beyond the borders of conventional religion's map.

Of course, the objective isn't just about acquiring more theology. What good would that be? Just fat heads and proud hearts. No, it's about revealing the surpassing goodness of our Father's heart and the richness of our identity in His eyes! The moment human hearts really realize that they are loved and secure in their Father's eyes, there is no stopping them. Better believing really does lead to better living.

Question: If you knew you didn't have to grovel or beg to receive and walk in Father's favor...how much time and spiritual energy would be freed up in your life? And we won't even mention your CPU bandwidth that so easily gets bogged down by sin management!

If you could be free of those oppressive weights, it would be like removing a 100-pound back pack off of your shoulders. You could run...you could fly...you're free! And this is just one of many discoveries you'll find herein.

Sonshift's ten chapters take you successively and succinctly through ten shifts, which is helpful not only the first time through, but also when you want to reference a specific point later.

True to Mel's style, he finds a kind of youthful mischievous delight in poking at sacred cows and traditional dogma. But he's fun and fresh enough in his presentation that even though you'll wince occasionally from his prodding, you'll be delighted when you discover that you also have become an iconoclast...and a part of the shift.

So, great job Mel. *Sonshift* is a huge asset to any searcher of current truth. It is presented well and with joy. Readers will feel challenged, enlightened, inspired and empowered...I certainly did.

Mark Hendrickson
Author of *Supernatural Provision*
Dwelling Place Ministries (DPM)
Kansas City, MO

INTRODUCTION

"Shift happens!" – Mark Hendrickson [1]

I wrote this book because something profound has happened to me, and is still happening.

My whole Christian worldview has been turned upside-down. I cannot read the Bible the same way I did for most of my previous thirty-something years with God, including faithfully serving as a leader and pastor of a local church.

Not that my identity and purpose have changed, but I am beginning to understand my identity and purpose *in Christ.* There has been a fundamental shift in my thinking on all fronts—how I see myself and how I relate to God and others. I have been shifted from living like a spiritual orphan to living like a beloved son in my heavenly Father's embrace. The rest of this book is devoted to explaining what that means.

But my personal story is not just my story. It represents what's happening to a growing number of God's beloved sons and daughters around the world today. So, perhaps this will be a confirmation for you, helping to explain what's going on in you. If not, may it serve as an invitation for you to be "shifted" too!

GOD NEVER CHANGES...BUT WE SHOULD

The Word of God never changes, but our understanding of God and His living Word *should* change. The Kingdom of God is always advancing, the increase of His government never ends.[2] That speaks of constant development and upgrade.

Indeed, we are told that we are to continue to grow *"till we all come to the unity of the faith and of the knowledge of the Son of God, to a perfect man, to the measure of the stature of the fullness of Christ..."* and that we *"may grow up in all things into Him who is the head—Christ."*[3] Frankly, I don't think we're there yet, do you?

I don't mean we should dismiss what has come before us, but we should build on the foundation of what is true in the revelation of Jesus Christ and leave behind what is not.

I am advocating being unafraid of change.

The problem is, we don't like change and we don't like leaving things in mystery. We studied and went to school so that we could have it all figured out, so we resist anyone who would propose that we haven't.

God seems to love change. Meaning, *our* change. And why wouldn't we *all* want this? Let me give you an illustration of what I mean.

Would you rather go to a sixteenth century doctor or a twenty-first century doctor for your ailments? Of course, you would want to benefit from the latest breakthroughs in medical advancement, right? Why, then, would you want to stay in a sixteenth century understanding of God and who you are in Him?

BEING KISSED AWAKE AFTER A LONG SLEEP

I often use fairytale analogies in this book to help tell the story of what has happened to me and what I see happening in the body of Christ. For instance, I see Jesus' bride—Sleeping Beauty—being kissed awake by her Beloved Prince after being lulled to sleep by the toxic poison of religious constructs born from the unrenewed mind of man rather than from the life of Christ in the Spirit.

I see the Church like an eagle mounting up on the foundation of what has come before, soaring into greater heights of freedom as she receives a better understanding of her identity, yet at the same time, becoming more grounded with childlike humility. This Bride is also less afraid because her heavenly Father's perfect love is driving out fear that had previously kept her bound. I see His love more intimately connecting us with each other.

Sonshift is not meant to be a theological treatise, although I do talk about theology, for I'm not primarily interested in reaching your head as much as I am in reaching your heart. In fact, I want your head to finally agree with your heart!

I'm also not attempting to make a doctrinal statement as much as I'm giving my own testimony and making an observation. In this light, I believe that we are currently in a major reformation. It's a major shift in thinking and relating to God as "Father" so profound that Christianity, and the way we view our relationship with Him, will never be the same.

AM I A SON OR A BRIDE?

My use of the word "son" and "bride" throughout this book may seem a bit confusing to some readers. Whenever "son" is used in the New Testament, it often indicates both sons and daughters. The Church is described as the "bride" of Christ in Scripture, which is made up of both men and women. These terms are not about gender but have to do with our relationship with God.

For instance, our relationship with our heavenly Father is like that of a son.[4] Our relationship with Jesus is like that of a bride.[5] Likewise, I'm using *Sonshift* to include sons and daughters.

GOD LIKES REFORMATION...ALL THE TIME

Jesus' first message was all about reformation.[6] The Greek word for "repent" (*metanoeō*) means to make a shift in thinking. This speaks of re-formation, whether it be personal or for a whole people group.

Jesus was essentially telling His Jewish brethren in Mark 1:15 to shift their thinking from offering bulls and goats as a way to get right with God to offering their hearts to Christ and believing Him by faith.

> *The kingdom they had been waiting for had finally come, but not as they expected. A similar disconnect is often true today.*

The kingdom they had been waiting for had finally come, but not as they expected. A similar disconnect is often true today.

This shift has been talked about by others in various ways but it bears repeating because it's vitally important that we see the big picture of what God is doing with His church in this hour.

Here's the way I see it. Starting from the Protestant Reformation until now, there have been three seismic shifts. I will call them reformations here. These shifts pertain to upgrades in how we relate to God, how we see ourselves as believers, and how we are to accomplish our mission on the earth. I believe that each shift builds on the foundation of the one before, so we can see them as a continual progression.

Here is a brief description of these three reformations.

The First Reformation (Jesus). Every Protestant Christian understands and agrees with this one. It started when Martin Luther nailed his famous "The Ninety-Five Theses on the Power and Efficacy of Indulgences" on the Wittenberg church door in 1517 and, thus, began what became the Protestant Reformation. The Church, as we know it, was changed forever and for the better in many ways.

The revelation was "justification by faith." The full authority of Scripture was re-established. The focus was on salvation by grace through faith alone. What was restored was a personal relationship with Jesus Christ. It was a type of a baptism in water.

The Second Reformation (Spirit). This reformation is a little more contested in the body of Christ. It began when Charles Parham and his little Bible study group in Topeka, Kansas, began speaking in tongues on January 1901. Through the Azusa Street Revival in Los Angeles that began in 1906, revival spread throughout the world. This was referred to as a Pentecostal movement. Later, in the 1960s, the Charismatic movement sprang from this well and touched all denominations in some way.

What was revealed was that the gifts of the Spirit, healing, and miracles are all for today. The authority of the believer over sickness and the powers of darkness was a focus of this reformation. What was restored was the personal relationship with the indwelling Holy Spirit *as a Person*. It was a type of a baptism of power.

The Third Reformation (Father). Even less understood and possibly more contested than the first two reformations is this third reformation that I alluded to earlier. It has to do with the Father's love. I believe it started in the 1970s with pioneers like Jack Winter, Doug Easterday, and Floyd McClung. But it was the "Toronto Blessing," as it was dubbed by the British newspapers, which launched it into worldwide fame in January of 1994.

What was revealed was the "Father Heart of God,"[7] that we have an abiding home in our Father's house, that He loves us as His adopted sons and daughters, and that we don't have to live like spiritual orphans anymore. What was restored was the personal relationship with God as a Father. It was (and is) all about our identification as His beloved sons and daughters. Many have described this reformation as a baptism of love.

Two quick observations I want to make about these three shifts. First, you can quickly tell which "reformation" that Christians and churches have camped around by what is emphasized, and more noticeably, by what they're against. Again, nobody really likes to change.

Second, I've noticed no discernible denominational (or non-denominational) tag coming from this current reformation of the Father's love. Much like what happened with the Charismatic movement, this move seems to affect all streams of the body of Christ. But much unlike the two former movements, this shift apparently brings us into genuine unity across these identification lines that would normally divide us.

> *While Jesus is the same, yesterday, today and forever, we are being changed from glory to glory.*

When we finally find our home in Papa's great big heavenly family, we no longer need to divide ourselves by our doctrines. *"Knowledge puffs up, but love edifies."*[8] Perhaps, we're starting to grow up! While Jesus is the same, yesterday, today and forever,[9] we are being changed from glory to glory.[10] And that's such a good thing.

SHARING MY TATTOOS

I tell the youth at my church that all my tattoos are on the inside. They come from God. Each encounter with Him has branded something deeply in my soul. And that's what this book is about. I'll share some of those "tattoos" with you as we take this journey together.

I wrote this book to testify how my utter failure to "act like a Christian" led to this shift. I'll share my story in the first chapter and throughout the book, of the failure of my old Christian paradigm to sustain my personal life, my marriage, and my life in general, and of my finding something altogether different and amazing.

I'll tell of Jesus walking right into my darkness full of abandonment, rejection, fear, shame, disappointment and regret, touching the cancer of my haunted soul and radiating it with His healing love.

LEGACY

This book is also about legacy. The dictionary defines legacy as something transmitted by or received from an ancestor or predecessor or from the past.

My wife, Maureen, and I were actually given this word, legacy, in 2007 at a conference in New Jersey. The prophetic team that was giving it saw baby cribs and baby bottles all around us and said that we would be helping people come into spiritual maturity, affecting generations to come. This was the beginning of a major shift in our ministry. A year later, the Lord spoke to me personally about raising up the next generation, which has been my focus since.

This would be the first of several pivotal prophetic words I received that provided insight to lead me where I am today. But I'm only one of many who have experienced such things, lending their voices for this generation and beyond. And many voices are needed for this shift to successfully take place.

Gradually, as I learned to be a son in my Father's embrace, I became a spiritual father. It is my sincere hope that, as I have soared beyond those who have poured their spiritual treasuries into me, you will take what I have learned and soar even higher. This is what inheritance and legacy are all about.

This book is also about legacy because it's for people I may never see—possibly a future generation who are not alive today. I hope people will read my book 50 years from now and marvel at how little we knew about the Kingdom. That's how it should be. Whatever the case, may the lessons learned here help you gain perspective and greater appreciation for what has come before you.

There's another way I hope to leave a legacy. I've witnessed the front end of two major moves of God in my lifetime. The first was about the restoration of the five-fold ministry and apostolic foundation in the church. Apostles (not writers of Scripture) once again became the equipping fathers and mothers of the local church and the foundation of local church government. I embraced this move as a young believer and have benefited greatly from this understanding.

The second move was about the Father's love (what I've called the third reformation). I was a pastor of a local church in a suburb of Chicago when it hit Toronto in 1994. Although I was a leader, I was still a spiritual orphan at this time, and I originally rejected what was going on because of the strange behavior that took place at these meetings.

Never judge something before you fully understand what God is doing.

I have since realized my rejection of these changes to be a big mistake that cost me several years of spiritual growth. While this was unfortunate, I did learn something valuable that I would like to pass on to you. Never judge something before you fully understand what God is doing. Give yourself time to assimilate the newness of it and give God time to speak to your heart.

Having gone through this process myself, I have a better understanding of people's resistance to change and the importance of staying humble and teachable in transition. I trust this piece of advice will be helpful to you as you read on.

THIS BOOK IS STILL BEING WRITTEN

While this shift is already happening in the body of Christ, it's still very much in transition. I'm still in transition myself as God continues to shift me personally. In fact, I trust there will be more things I will have learned by the time you've read this book. And, hopefully, you are constantly learning and changing, too.

Sonshift is about a life in process, but never lived apart from the Father's embrace. It's about actually knowing and believing the following promise of the Father:

I will not in any degree leave you helpless nor forsake nor let you down (relax My hold on you)! Assuredly not! (Heb.13:5b AMP)

HOW THIS BOOK IS LAID OUT

I know that many don't actually read books from cover to cover. For this reason, I've made it easier for you by arranging it so that it can be digested in various ways.

There are ten chapters of various lengths in this book that show the different areas where God has shifted my view of my life in Christ. While each chapter can stand on its own, if you want to skip around, it is probably best read in order for context and a fuller understanding. I do suggest that you read the first chapter titled, "What is Sonshift?" first. This chapter will give you an overview of what the whole book is about.

Finally, I would like to mention before we get started that I write extensively about this subject on my blog at melwild.wordpress.com. I invite you to check it out and join in the conversation too!

Shall we begin?

INTRODUCTION ENDNOTES

[1] From Mark Hendrickson's blog post, "The Changing Face of Christianity." Retrieved at https://marklhen.wordpress.com/2013/08/31/the-changing-face-of-christianity/

[2] Isaiah 9:7

[3] Ephesians 4:13, 15

[4] See Romans 8:14, 19; Galatians 3:26; 4:5-6; Ephesians 1:5; Hebrews 2:10

[5] See Matthew 9:15; 25:1; Ephesians 5:25, 31-32; Revelation 18:23; 21:2; 22:17

[6] See Mark 1:15. Young's Literal Translation (YLT) renders it this way, "...Reform ye, and believe in the good news." Reformation is another way of understanding repentance.

[7] The "Father Heart of God" term was used by Doug Easterday with a training class by the same title with Youth With a Mission (YWAM), going back to 1979. Floyd McClung also wrote a book by the same title (Harvest House pub., May 1985)

[8] 1 Corinthians 8:1

[9] See Hebrews 13:8

[10] See 2 Corinthians 3:18

WHAT IS SONSHIFT?

"When will my daughter waken?" said the Queen.
"I don't know," the fairy admitted sadly. "In a year's time,
ten years or twenty?" the Queen went on. "Maybe in a hun-
dred years' time. Who knows?" said the fairy. "Oh! What
would make her waken?" asked the Queen weeping. "Love,"
replied the fairy. "If a man of pure heart were to fall in love
with her that would bring her back to life!"

– From Sleeping Beauty [1]

You and I are Sleeping Beauty.

Not the Sleeping Beauty of the Brothers Grimm story but the object of God's deepest affection in His ultimate love story. Unlike the fairytale, His romantic tale is true.

Sonshift is about my personal journey into the Father's heart and how that has changed everything—how I see God and my relationship to Him, how I relate to my family and friends, how I read the Bible, and even the foundational things that I thought made up the Christian life.

Sonshift is about Jesus' true love—His Sleeping Beauty—in the middle of a great awakening. She isn't dead, just sleeping. She's always been just as beautiful as she was on the day she was born. Jesus has always loved her the same. But a wicked prince has always hated her *because* she is the object of the King's deepest affection. So he tried to kill her, but he could only manage to put her in an orphan sleep. And now, in our lifetime, the time has come for her to awaken.

ENJOYING OUR LIVES MORE THAN SINNERS

James Jordan said something profound recently at a conference. It captures what this current shift is all about.

> I believe we are seeing today a unique day in the body of Christ. I believe we're living in a day unprecedented since the days of the apostles. We're living in a day where God is revealing Himself to us as Father. And because the Father is love, His love is becoming available to us like it hasn't been for 2,000 years. And as that love is coming, it's turning our Bibles upside down, inside-out, back to front. It is turning our Christianity, upside-down, inside-out, back to front. It is, for the first time, putting us in the place where we can enjoy our life more than sinners.[2]

This statement is both profoundly exciting and sad at the same time. It's exciting because we're living in a day unprecedented since the apostles. But sad because we're only just getting to the place where we can *enjoy our lives more than sinners*. But, praise God, to quote the poet prophet from the 1960s, Bob Dylan—*the times they are a changing!*

Sonshift is exactly what James Jordan was talking about, the turning of our understanding of Christianity upside-down, inside-out and back-to-front. It's what happens when we find ourselves caught up in the Father's unfathomable ocean of love, buoyed and empowered by the scandalous grace that comes through Jesus Christ.

A NEW EXPRESSION HAS COME!

A few years ago, I first came upon the following prophetic word from Mike Bickle. He said that he got this word in 1982 while in Cairo, Egypt. It was so powerful that he said the Lord spoke to him in an audible voice. Bickle reported hearing the following: *"The Spirit said, 'I will change the understanding and expression of Christianity on earth in one generation.'"* [3]

The first time I read this, I was stunned! I said to myself, *"This is exactly what has been happening to me!"* And now I know it's happening to all of us, whether we've realized it or not, for I believe that we are that generation. God has been awakening His Bride to the Father's love, and we're just beginning to learn how to have the heart of the Father and see everything through His eyes just like Jesus did.

> *Sonshift is about Jesus' true love—His Sleeping Beauty—in the middle of a great awakening.*

We're finally seeing the truth, no longer seeing ourselves separated from Him as "dirty sinners" with "filthy rags" righteousness. Now we know that we have HIS righteousness because we died *with* Him and our life is now Christ's life.[4] We're beginning to see our true identity as the Father's "pearl of great price," for He is the "merchant" who gave what was most valuable to Him to purchase us.[5]

We are finally seeing that we're not like spiritual beggars living under a bridge, hoping God will look our way and give us some crumbs from His table. We're royal sons and daughters living in the palace of the Great King! With this position comes great favor and responsibility.

We're finally seeing that we've been invited into something most wonderful! It's what Dr. C. Baxter Kruger so beautifully describes as the Great Dance, *"the unchained communion and intimacy, fired by passionate, self-giving and other-centered love, and mutual delight,"*[6] and that it's been going on since before time began.

It's about time we see this because here's the sad truth about our influence on the earth today: while the people you and I live around don't seem to have a problem with Jesus, they have a huge problem with His body—the Church. How can this be if we're supposed to be *as He is* in this world?[7] Something is terribly amiss in our understanding of the Christian life.

As strange as it may seem, people's rejection of Christianity is not because of Jesus' message. It's because of *our message*. The offense is not so much with the cross of Christ, it's in *our packaging* of the cross of Christ. It's because we've made God in our own broken image.

> *Something is terribly amiss in our understanding of the Christian life.*

Still, in spite of all of this, I see the Church moving into a fresh wave of reformation. To use my fairytale analogy, I see Jesus' beautiful bride—Sleeping Beauty—being kissed awake by her Beloved Prince after being lulled to sleep by the toxic poison of religion. It's a glorious time to be alive!

This would be a good place for me share a little of my own awakening.

A NEW LIFE AND A WIFE!

I still remember that warm summer night in 1978, sitting on a bluff overlooking the Mississippi River, where I gave my heart to Jesus. I had always believed in God but had long rejected the Catholic religion of my youth. As a young adult, I had sought after my own counterfeit affections, awash in my prodigal world of "sex, drugs, and rock & roll."

But my story is not about someone desperately hanging at the end of their rope and crying out to Jesus to rescue them from certain doom. No, I was actually pretty happy with my life. At least, as I understood happiness at the time.

I had been having a conversation on that particular river bluff that night with my future wife, Maureen, whom I had just recently met. I was a musician living in Austin, Texas, at the time but was home visiting my mother in Iowa. Maureen happened to be living in my hometown, and we met at a party after I played a gig with a makeshift band put together with some of my old friends. She didn't normally go to these kinds of parties, but apparently had come to hear us play with her sister and was introduced to me through a mutual friend. We talked quite a while at the party, and I was almost instantly infatuated and love struck! Joyfully, I found out later that the infatuation was mutual.

However, there was something else going on that night on the river bluff. Maureen kept talking about Jesus *as if she actually knew Him*. She was so different than the "Jesus freaks" I had occasionally run into since the early '70s. (That's a whole other story!) This was no canned Roman's Road, "come to Jesus or else" speech. She was speaking with great familiarity and intimacy from a heart full of love and devotion.

It became obvious to me that I was missing something wonderful, and I wanted to know Him, too, so right there…no altar call, no sinner's prayer…just a beautiful moonlit night with a beautiful woman…I decided to give my life to Jesus so that I could know Him like she did. And He took me up on the invitation big time. That night, I threw away my counterfeit high for the Most High!

Suddenly, I was radically infected and intoxicated with Jesus!

I would often be found driving down the road in my old boxy Ford station wagon, screaming out the words to "Amazing Grace" while crying and laughing at the same time. I was a sight! It was like my whole world went from black and white to color.

I couldn't get enough of this Jesus. (Or my future wife!)

The longer story involved me staying in Iowa the whole summer, moving back from Texas, getting to know Maureen better and eventually moving to Chicago (her hometown), going to school, enjoying my new life, and getting married in the fall of 1980.

In 1982, we got involved in a local church. Together, we went to Bible studies and conferences and learned how to operate in the gifts of the Spirit. It was amazing. I made some wonderful friends and learned so much about God.

Then something terrible happened.

GIVING MY LIFE TO JESUS BUT LOSING MY SOUL

Unfortunately, as I started to live my new life in Christ I also learned what was wrong with everything. Instead of continuing to bask in God's love and grace as I had when I first met Jesus, my Christianity gradually became more and more about sin management and behavior modification.

I learned about who to stay away from, what to fear about this wicked world, how to watch out for all those false teachers, cults, the government, the antichrist, wrong movies, evil music. But even more frightening, I learned that God knew all my secret sins and was generally NOT happy with me. At least, that's how I understood it.

From my new viewpoint as a Christian, the Good News certainly wasn't giving me great joy.

I was ordained in 1991 to become part of a pastoral team in a local church in a Chicago suburb. Now I was a leader! *But where would I lead anyone?* You can't take someone somewhere you've never been yourself. So I led people from my limited experience and accumulation of intellectual knowledge. I parroted sound bites I had learned from preachers I listened to, but with little intimate knowledge of Him.

Slowly, almost methodically, the innocent childlike joy went away. Much like the Ephesian church in Revelation, I had all the right answers, knew who all the bad guys were, but I had lost my first love.

I realize now that I went from being the prodigal son to being the elder brother! As Leif Hetland[8] would say, I traded my rebellion for religion. I lost even the level of joy and happiness I once had as a sinner (remember the James Jordan quote).

Actually, I secretly wished I could still do a lot of the things I used to do in my former life, and I subconsciously resented God for taking these "fun" things away. My heart was in hiding, certainly not in sync with what I thought I knew was right.

Oh, I knew a lot about what the Bible says because I studied it in-cessantly. I was discipled by the best, was trained, led Bible studies, preached sermons, read all the books, went to conferences, watched Christian TV...and as years went by, I found talk radio and 24-hour news channels where I could stay angry on a steady diet of what was wrong with everything else in the evil world I was warned not to love.

Sadly, I had become a master at hiding my own sin while confess-ing everyone else's. I could parrot all the right Christian jingles on com-mand (like *"God is good...all the time!"*), but I knew nothing about the Father's heart, or about how to open my own heart to love and inti-macy. I could never really see His goodness.

I identified myself as a so-called "Spirit-filled" Charismatic be-liever, which meant I believed in the gifts of Spirit and doing the "stuff." I often used these things to prove my worth and looked down on those who didn't believe in or do such things. What I saw as being a level-headed, spiritually mature, and discerning man of God was ac-tually being a self-righteous and judgmental hypocrite. In reality, my heart was more like that of a Charismatic Pharisee than a Charismatic Jesus.

Then, in 1995, the "Toronto Blessing"[9] hit the Chicago area. I went with a couple of our other leaders to a big meeting in one of the churches in the suburbs to get a taste of the experience. I was immedi-ately offended. People were rolling on the floor, racing around the room, barking like dogs, some passed out for hours. It was total chaos! I thought to myself, *"This is a circus!"* And maybe it was...on the out-side looking in. The truth was, even though I considered myself a "Spirit-filled Charismatic," the only gifts I seemed to be operating in at the time were the gifts of suspicion and criticism!

I was a blind fool who was totally ignorant of what the Father was doing with His children because I thought I had "discernment." Sure, there were excesses that were not God, but I realize now that what I called discernment was really spiritual arrogance and ignorance, and it cost me several years of real spiritual progress because I let my religious pride lead me away from an opportunity to get back the tender love I once had, that I could've experienced anew, had I let my heart be open to something that, at first, didn't seem "normal."

Instead, I continued down my self-righteous path as a spiritual orphan for several more years. Nonetheless, I have found that God is faithful. He will never leave you, but He will let you keep going around the same mountain just as long as you want!

So like the Grinch who stole Christmas, my heart grew very small.

I had given my life to Jesus but had lost my soul. The rich vibrant tones of my life became a religious pallor. I became rigid, stoic, and Spock-like. I traded the wild wonder of God's love and sometimes scary freedom, for a safe religious world that I could control, one guided by my own human limitations and reason. Doctrine and God's Word became my god instead of the God of the Word.

Then, something truly wonderful happened!

MY GLORIOUS CRASH

My life came to a resounding crash as summer came to a close in 2001. I like to say that I had my own personal 9/11. It was the beginning of a glorious awakening but at the time it felt like I had fallen into the pit of hell.

By this time I had become cynical, unfaithful, full of shame and self-loathing and mad at God. My marriage was basically over, especially after my wife found out I was trying to have a relationship with another woman. Thankfully, I failed in that foolish endeavor, too.

I was bi-vocational at the time: my previously very successful business was failing miserably, my three sons were in high school by now, I had no way of putting them through college, and I was in trouble with the IRS to boot. Because of all of this, we were losing the very nice home we built in the country and going bankrupt. Somewhere in my self-absorbed version of Christianity, I felt God must be at fault for all my problems.

I didn't even want to get out of bed in the morning. I felt paralyzed with fear and totally alone, just like I had felt many times when I was growing up. All of my old demons had come rushing back into my life.

There was nothing that was working...except this glorious crash.

I think my theme song at the time could have been Bob Dylan's, *"Everything is Broken!"*[10] Added to all of this, I felt like a total hypocrite and failure as a leader. Why should anyone listen to me? I felt such deep shame.

Little did I suspect at the time that I was about to encounter this Father of love like I had never known Him before!

Now I know it was my foolishness that had just blown up my world, and God's mercy would use my mess for my good, but little did I suspect at the time that I was about to encounter this Father of love like I had never known Him before!

I think the Message Bible describes best what was about to happen to me...

> *You're blessed when you feel you've lost what is most dear to you. Only then can you be embraced by the One most dear to you. (Matt. 5:4 MSG)*

I remember this moment in my life vividly, as if it were happening right now. The terrorists of my soul who had lured my orphan heart into this darkness had now flown their planes into my flimsy religious house of cards and it was burning down. My wife had left me a note saying she was leaving me because of the other woman, my business had failed—even my "Christianity" had come crashing down into a rubbly heap that smoldered in the dungeon of my torment.

At the same time, I could hear the siren song of the freedom of my old life as a carefree musician with no one to answer to but my own self-indulgence.

It was at this moment, seemingly suspended in time and space, that I heard God speak to my heart, *"Now's your chance. You can pursue the life you've always wanted, the one you gave up for Me, and the reason why you think you hate Me right now.* (I had been mad at God for over a year by then and even refused to pray to Him.)

> *Then, something in me, most unexpectedly, miraculously, chose to face my hell with Him.*

He continued, *"Nothing is stopping you now…not your wife, not your business, and certainly not your position in the church…you are free."*

As I look back at this now, it reminds me of when Jesus turned to His disciples, after having thousands walk away from Him when He gave His *"unless you drink my blood and eat my flesh"* speech, and asked them if they wanted to leave Him, too. I know now what they meant when they said, *"Lord, where would we go? You have the words that give eternal life."*[11]

You see, love requires real freedom of choice. And only free people can truly love each other. I didn't know that at the time, but I was about to find out! God was giving me a choice. And that choice was very real to me. It was between having the freedom to run away from my marriage, all my failings, *from Him*…or do the worst thing I could possibly imagine at the time—let go of my pride and face this hell *with* Him. I hope you understand, I truly felt like I was living in hell. Then, something in me, most unexpectedly, miraculously, chose to face my hell with Him.

Somewhere in my heart I heard the words, *I don't care if I lose everything*—and I certainly thought I had—*I don't want to lose You.*

Let me say here that there are many things you find out in life that you never knew that you didn't know. You don't even have a mental grid to ask the right question. What I was about to experience was one of those times! I was about to be introduced to a ridiculously loving Father who I had never known all my natural life, all my Christian life.

THE SHIFT!

Although I didn't have understanding of what was going on in me at that time, from the moment I decided to face my hell with God, I suddenly felt my heavenly Father's BIG arms of love around me, hugging all the vitriolic poison out of my soul. He just kept hugging me and hugging me. I would just sit there and cry with tears of joy. And this healing process went on for many months.

Please understand, in my whole life I had never been hugged even once by my biological father, so this was *so*...wonderfully foreign to me. This is what I now call living in the Father's embrace.

I got my soul back. Love had awakened me!

I can happily tell you now that I have never loved God more passionately than I do now. My whole world was turned upside down that day. Or, should I say, turned right side up. I was able to love again because I was finally able to receive love from Love.

I did lose my house and my business, but not what really mattered—my wife and my family. I love my wife more than ever! She is so beautiful and brilliant to me now. We miraculously got back together and renewed our wedding vows on our 21st anniversary in October of 2001. As of this writing, we've been married for 35 years. We still have our ups and downs, but nothing like before. And I can truly say that I've gained a love for people... all of them...even the seemingly worst of them.

But most importantly, I gained revelation of a life I always possessed but never knew—a life filled with the Father's love.

I pray that my story will encourage you. I'll be transparent and say I don't feel the Father's embrace all the time and my life is still far from perfect, but I *do* have joy again! More importantly, I know where to find His embrace and joy whenever I need it. My world is in brilliant color again.

I don't just read the Bible for information but to encounter the Word in God's word. It's truly living and breathing in the deepest part of my soul. My spirit soars in the highest heavenly realm with my Father! I can feel Jesus' pulsating grace constantly flooding and overflowing my heart. I'm not afraid of or mad at the world anymore, for His love is conquering all my fear. He will most certainly do the same for you.

CAN WE JUST ADMIT THAT OUR CURRENT MODEL IS BROKEN?

Let me say very frankly that our current popular packaging of Christianity is broken. Maybe it should be. It's not very attractive and it has not really been good news. Our manipulative, fear-mongering version of an "angry god" gospel worked, somewhat, centuries ago when people were obsessed with Dante-like images of hellfire and brimstone. It doesn't work now.

Ironically, this was also true in Jesus day.

Sinners loved Jesus because He really loved them. They didn't love the religious leaders because the religious leaders didn't really love them.

Bill Johnson says something very true about this, *"Everyone wants a King like Jesus. And if we will represent Him well, they'll want His body, too."*[12]

I believe this present shift is changing how this world—a world that the Father loves so much that He bankrupted heaven—will see His beloved sons and daughters. They will see this because we have been "shifted" by God, both in our view of our relationship with Him and in how we see others through Him.

Sonshift is about an awakening. Even more than this, it's about the continuing reformation of His Church. It's the progressive awakening to the bigger, ultimate purpose for which God created us in the first place, *"having predestined us to adoption as sons by Jesus Christ to Himself, according to the good pleasure of His will."*[13] In other words, our heavenly Father wants a people, fully alive in His embrace, walking out their lives as fully-affirmed sons and daughters. And He won't stop until we look, think, and act exactly like Jesus!

THE SPIRITUAL ORPHAN MINDSET

Since this whole book is about the paradigm shift from thinking like a spiritual orphan to thinking like a son, I should probably take some time to summarize what I mean by spiritual orphan. I will explain most of the following points in greater detail throughout the book.

First, a spiritual orphan, in a word, is about *separation*. By definition, orphans are fatherless. Spiritual orphans also live unmindful of being in the constant embrace of their heavenly Father. Their language and how they see and talk about God all reveals this disconnect. While they agree that they are in Christ, God, for them, is up in heaven somewhere while they are on the earth. Therefore, the spiritual orphan mindset is about the *illusion of separation.*

Much of our current popular religious mindset contradicts the truth about who we are in Christ

Orphan theology is always about distance and delay.

Orphan revivals are about begging God to come down and visit instead of walking in an everyday revival lifestyle where they are empowered by His incarnated life in them.

Any time you view yourself separate from God in any way, you are thinking like a spiritual orphan. It was true that from Adam until Christ we *were* separated from God because the first orphan, Satan, got Adam to eat from the wrong tree. But Jesus, the first and only begotten Son, told us in John 14:18 that when He left He would not leave us as spiritual orphans anymore.

I will not leave you orphans; I will come to you.

Jesus promised that, by sending us His Spirit, He and His Father would come and make their home in us.[14] By the Father and Jesus coming to make their home in us via the Spirit, we are no longer orphans but adopted sons. This is what Paul is telling us.

> *And because you are sons, God has sent forth the Spirit of His Son into your hearts, crying out, "Abba, Father!" (Gal.4:6)*

Jesus, in His final discourse in the gospel of John (John 13:31-17:26), before He was betrayed by the spiritual orphans of His day, told us about what it looks like when you're at home in the Father and He's at home in you.

This discourse needs to be read as one message. It's about our life with our Father in Christ as a son in the Spirit.

We don't have to wait for the "sweet by and by" to be home. The stunning reality is, you *are* home—*now*—in Him, whether you know it or not. Our inability to understand this heavenly reality gets to the heart of the problem.

We've been taught and have lived with an orphan view of Christianity for many centuries. We've inherited a theology that's more like the old covenant than the new. Once you see it, you will clearly see that much of our current popular religious mindset contradicts the truth about who we are in Christ.

The risk I take in saying all of this is that this mindset is so deeply entrenched in your thinking (and has been in mine) that you may dismiss or argue with what I'm saying before asking God if it's actually true. This is because we tend to think that everything we believe is the truth, and anyone who disagrees with us is wrong.

In addition to this, we just don't know what we don't know. But I'm getting ahead of myself. For now, I just ask that you stay open to what I'm saying and give the Holy Spirit time to give you revelation.

Here are some examples of what I mean by this orphan-hearted illusion of separation. These points will also be covered in more detail in the subsequent chapters.

We are thinking like a spiritual orphan when...

...we see Jesus crucified, buried and resurrected but we don't see *ourselves* crucified, buried and resurrected *in* Him.

...it's all about going to heaven when we die instead of being invited into fellowship with the Father in the Son at His right hand in heaven now.[15]

...we relate to Jesus more than the Father, even though Jesus' purpose was to bring us into the *same relationship* He has had with the Father from eternity.[16]

...we think, and even say, that Jesus is the only way to heaven when He thought and said that He was the only way *to the Father*.[17]

...we pray "begging" prayers, asking God to do something He told us to do or has already done, instead of "declarative" prayers of faith based in Christ's finished work on the cross.

...we sing songs asking the Holy Spirit to "come" instead of asking to be made more aware of His presence already in us.

...we prefer the things of God *apart* from Him rather than having them *in* Him, like the younger rebellious brother.[18]

...we put off our inheritance until we die and go to heaven, never availing ourselves of all that the Father has now, like the elder religious brother.[19]

...we think we're getting a "mansion" up in the sky somewhere when we die instead of it being a dwelling place in the Spirit now.[20]

...we see ourselves as a slave instead of a son,[21] a servant of God instead of His friend and confidential partner[22] serving all people.

...our relationship with God is shaped more by duty and obligation than by intimacy and mutually reciprocating love.

...we say (or sing) that *this is not our home,* and that heaven is our home, but we fail to see that we're living *from* heaven now.[23]

...we relate more to the Old Covenant of conditional outward performance than the unconditional love, righteousness and holiness freely given to us through the grace of Jesus Christ.[24]

...we're seeing ourselves *in any way* different than *as Christ in this world.*[25] Not that we're God, but that His life is our life.[26]

There are more, but you get the idea.

This orphan mindset was seen in the carnal, earthbound Corinthians in Paul's day, who he called "spiritual infants" because they were thinking like "mere humans." How were they doing this? By dividing themselves by their pet doctrines and by whom they followed.[27]

In other words, when we think being a "____" (fill in your denomination or non-denomination) is more important than being part of the whole family of God on the earth, we reveal this orphan mindset.

Furthermore, spiritual orphans don't think multi-generationally, but think only for themselves. They prefer doctrines that feed their need for self-preservation.

Also, spiritual orphans don't consider the original, unrescinded mandate for dominion,[28] which was to cultivate the culture of heaven on the earth—to represent the Father's heart as Jesus did, until the knowledge of God covers the earth like the waters cover the sea.[29]

Like the Gnostics of old, religious orphans would rather condemn this physical planet and escape from it than be the light and love of our Father in it.

We *are* fully-affirmed sons and daughters of our heavenly Father—not scared and fear-driven victims groping in the dark. We belong to one another, part of the biggest family in creation, spanning both heaven and earth.

Let's stop thinking like orphans, praying like orphans, singing like orphans, and be about our Father's business. He's got really good things in mind for us!

IS GOD REVEALING OUR TRUE COLORS?

Maureen shared something with me about autumn leaves that made me think about what God is doing in this hour. We live in an area that is absolutely beautiful in the autumn. Besides our many rivers, hills, and majestic soaring bald eagles, the leaves turn brilliant colors of red, orange, and yellow.

What she pointed out to me is that these beautiful colors are actually the leaves' true colors. In other words, green is not their true color. Doing a little research, I found this to be true. Here's an excerpt from an article by Heather Rhoades on the subject:

> As the days get shorter, the tree does not have enough sunlight to make food for itself. Rather than struggle to make food through the winter, it shuts down. It stops producing chlorophyll and allows its fall leaves to die. When the tree stops producing chlorophyll, the green color leaves the foliage and you are left with the "true color" of the leaves.[30]

Leaves are naturally red, orange and yellow. The green just normally covers this up. What's interesting to me about this is that what is hidden is revealed in full maturity. This made me think of how Paul tells us that all of creation is waiting for the sons of God to be revealed. Let's look at this verse for a moment:

> *For the earnest expectation of the creation eagerly waits for the **revealing** of the **sons** of God. (Rom. 8:19)*

There are two words here in the original Greek we should consider more closely.

Revealing – (*apokalypsis*) besides meaning appearance, can also mean a disclosure, revelation, spiritual enlightenment.

Sons – (*hyios*) means a son as implying connection in respect of membership, service, resemblance, manifestation, or destiny.

Could it be that this "revealing" has to do with spiritual enlightenment, disclosure and revelation about connection, resemblance and destiny? And if this is true, to whom is this being revealed? Could it be to you and me?

Could this mean that the sons of God are revealed when they accept what God says about them, coming forth as a *unique race of beings* (Greek word for "new" is *kainos* – of a unique order, unprecedented – see 2 Cor. 5:17), and take hold of their true identity by faith, walking in the authority and power of their Father in heaven of which Christ is the firstborn?[31]

> *Beloved of God, is all of creation waiting for you and me to see our true colors?*

Why is this understanding important? Because even though we *already* are fully-authorized sons and daughters of God, we may not know it. An orphan may be biologically born of a king yet live like a homeless beggar. Then, after many years, the king's messenger may search him out, and when he finally finds him, he reveals his true identity to him. This revelation will forever change the life of the son, although it may take some time for his "beggar" mindset to change. This is what this revealing means.

I believe we're waking up from centuries of homeless beggar religion, one that we've called the Christian life, to the glory and power of *His* life, the royal life we were created for, because the King's messenger—His Spirit—has sought us out in order to bring out our true colors.

Beloved of God, is all of creation waiting for you and me to see our true colors? To come into maturity, finally seeing our inseparable connection and resemblance to our heavenly Father?

I do believe we are living in a day where we're finally leaving this darkened mindset of orphan-hearted religion that separates us from God. We're finally learning how to live the exchanged life in our heavenly Father's embrace—where we love like Him, talk like Him, see like Him—bringing His splendor, His magnificence and His glory everywhere we walk on this earth. And this reality is absolutely stunning to behold!

> *"Arise, shine; for your light has come, and the glory of the Lord has risen upon you. "For behold, darkness will cover the earth and deep darkness the peoples; but the Lord will rise upon you and His glory will appear upon you. "Nations will come to your light, and kings to the brightness of your rising. (Isa. 60:1-3 NASB)*

CHAPTER ONE ENDNOTES

[1] Grimm, *Sleeping Beauty*. Quote retrieved at http://www.yankeeweb.com/library/storytime/grimmbros/grimmbros_56.html

[2] James Jordan, Fatherheart Ministries. From "What Christianity is, and is not" - retrieved at http://youtu.be/IuTW8Ht3WcU .

[3] Mike Bickle, Founder of International House of Prayer – Kansas City. A copy of this prophecy can be found at http://www.ihopkc.org/anniversary/

[4] See Galatians 2:20; Colossians 3:3; 2 Corinthians 5:21

[5] See Matthew 13:45-46; John 3:16.

[6] From C. Baxter Kruger's blog post titled, "Summary of the Trinitarian Vision." Retrieved at http://baxterkruger.blogspot.com/2012/09/summary-of-trinitarian-vision.html.

[7] 1 John 4:17

[8] Leif Hetland, founder of Global Mission Awareness.

[9] "Toronto Blessing," as it was dubbed by the British newspapers, was a revival that hit the Toronto Airport Vineyard Church in January of 1994.

[10] Dylan, "Everything is Broken" © 1989 by Special Rider Music.

[11] John 6:68 ERV

[12] Bill Johnson, author and apostolic leader based out of the Bethel Church in Redding, California.

[13] Ephesians 1:5

[14] See John 14:23

[15] 1 John 1:3-5

[16] See John 17:21-26

[17] See John 14:6

[18] See Luke 15:11-24

[19] See Luke 12:32; 15:31

[20] See John 14:2-3, 18, 23; 17:21-26

[21] See Galatians 4:7

[22] See John 15:15

[23] See Ephesians 2:6; Philippians 3:20; Hebrews 12:22

[24] See John 1:16-17
[25] See 1 John 4:17
[26] See Galatians 2:20; Colossians 3:3
[27] See 1 Corinthians 1:10-13; 3:1-3
[28] Genesis 1:26-28
[29] See Habakkuk 2:4
[30] Article by Heather Rhoades, "Fall Leaf Life Cycle: Why Do Leaves Change Colors In The Autumn." Retrieved at http://www.gardening-knowhow.com/ornamental/trees/tgen/fall-leaf-life-cycle-why-do-leaves-change-colors-in-the-autumn.htm
[31] See Romans 8:29; Colossians 1:18

CHAPTER TWO

FATHER SHIFT

Oh, Father, dear Father! Have I found you at last?
Now I shall never, never leave you again!
It is I! Look at me! And you have forgiven me, haven't you?
Oh, my dear Father, how good you are!

- Pinocchio [1]

Geppetto was certainly not a perfect example of a good father. In fact, fairytales rarely, if ever, portray a good father.

This is the same problem we have in the real world. We rarely see good father examples. Yet, everything good in this life actually finds its source from our heavenly Father whether we know it or not, so we must realize at the outset that what truly makes a good father is a reflection of Him.[2]

A lot of the details of this particular fairytale won't hold true to my point, but one thing about Geppetto that has our heavenly Father's fingerprints all over it was his undying love for Pinocchio. Our heavenly Father's one burning desire for us, like Geppetto's burning desire for Pinocchio, is that we would be His son forever.

Another heavenly connection we can make is that Pinocchio finds His father in the middle of his darkest hell...in the belly of a shark. Like

Pinocchio, we find that our heavenly Father has come to live right in the middle of the darkest part of us, too.

In the story, our wooden protagonist spent his life much like the prodigal son of Scripture—leaving his father and going into a far country to chase after counterfeit pleasures that would never give him the life he really wanted. It wasn't until he came to the end of himself that he found out what really mattered—his father's affirming love.

A PERSONAL ENCOUNTER WITH PAPA GOD

When God the Father reveals Himself to you in a personal way, not only do you see Him for who He really is, you begin to see yourself as who you really are in Him.

Since my glorious crash in 2001, I've had many such encounters with my heavenly Papa. One was during a SOZO[3] session several years ago. I mentioned to the ministry team that I had been wondering why I always prayed to Jesus but almost never to the Father. I also expressed some frustration that my worship experience seemed to stop short.

As we prayed, I asked the Father to show me what was going on. I was immediately brought to a time when I was about six or seven years old. I was in the living room of my house and I had innocently jumped on my sleeping father's lap and woke him up. Because he was sleeping, I startled him and he reacted angrily. He was rarely home when I was growing up so I was anxious to show him something. I don't even remember what it was and I hadn't even thought about this incident at all until this session.

During this session, I realized for the first time that I had taken his normal, startled response as a rejection, and it had become part of how I saw myself. This greatly affected my ability to show affection, especially in my relationship to my heavenly Father. The SOZO team leader asked me to see if the Father had anything to tell me now about this incident. I closed my eyes again and immediately got a vision of the same green chair that my dad had been sleeping in, only this time it was much taller and extremely bright. All I could see at first were beams of light coming from the chair. Then I saw what I perceived to be my heavenly Father looking down and smiling at me.

I saw *Him*! And He was smiling...*at me!*

Then I saw Him gesture to me to jump up on His lap. He said, *"You can jump in my lap anytime, day or night...I will always be here waiting. And I will never tell you to get off"*

I was undone.

To say words are inadequate is a major understatement. I'll never be able to describe the experience or what the experience did *in* me. All I can say is that my relationship with my heavenly Papa immediately changed and has never been the same since.

Now, every time I close my eyes and open my heart to Him, I see Him smiling with arms open wide, waiting for me to jump on His lap! And I do. *This* is how I worship now. I close my eyes...*and jump.*

Not only did my worship experience change, I saw myself differently, too. This encounter, and many others like it, have helped to shape my view of God, my theology, and my understanding of my identity in Him.

This is what our Papa God does. He picks us up and lovingly affirms us as His son or daughter. His intention is for us to live continuously under His smile. It's not that He doesn't correct us as a good father does, but now I never see it as the rejection or punishment I did when I was a spiritual orphan. Now I see it as a point of discovery in my experience in Him. I love His correction because it always means upgrade!

Beloved, He's given us His Spirit of adoption.[4] He drapes the royal robe over our prodigal heart, puts the signet ring on our judgmental finger, and sandals on our runaway feet and says, *"Welcome home! Let's party!"*

Another thing that changed from these encounters with my Father is that now my heart beats with *His* love. Papa is teaching me how to love like Him, and my burning desire is to bring the spiritual orphan home to my Father's House, to be embraced as sons and daughters in His big family.

COMING OUT OF MY FATHERLESS PAST

The incident described above wasn't the only wound I had been unknowingly carrying, and God has healed me of so many wounds over the years. I share my story to perhaps help you see something in your own life that was never the Father's intention for you. He is a father, which means He is always about family. But maybe your story is similar to mine in that you might've thought what you grew up with was "normal" and now you don't understand what's going on inside of you.

For some, it may be that you had a father at home but he was verbally or physically abusive. Maybe he was a good father but he just didn't show much affection—he was distant, or maybe you felt like you had to win his approval. Even if you had a great dad, he probably wasn't perfect.

The problem is, all of these factors affect how we relate to our heavenly Father. My father was never abusive, he was just absent most of the time. Though I never realized it at the time, looking back now, I understand how inadequate and insecure I felt growing up. My friends all seemed to know how to do the "guy" things. I grew up in a time when most fathers were at home. They showed their sons how to fix things, "be a man" and take responsibility. I could only guess at what that meant. My father showed me that he had another, more important, life elsewhere and I was left to fend for myself.

I'm not pointing a finger at my father to assess blame; I'm pointing this out to say that I grew up to be just like him. I carried this "normal" into my adulthood, into my prodigal world. I grew up closed off to intimacy and trust, looking for love but keeping everyone at a safe distance. I would have to say that, at that time, my relationships with others could best be described as being alone together.

As I shared in the first chapter, I met and fell in love with Maureen and we married in 1980. Our first child came in 1982. Suddenly, I was a father and all the old inadequacies and insecurities come rushing back in. *I don't know how to be a father!* Anger began to build up inside of me at having to learn everything I was supposed to know already but was never taught, though I never let it come to the surface. At least, at first.

Fortunately, Maureen's father was an excellent role model and I learned a lot about how be a dad from him. I also had great spiritual fathers who started to pour their lives into me. I kept my anger at bay, but it was still a very rough journey for me as I struggled for years with intimacy issues with those closest to me and especially with God.

HOW DO YOU SEE YOUR HEAVENLY FATHER?

Before we move on, I would like you to close your eyes for a minute and try to picture your heavenly Father. How do you "see" Him? What do you think HE thinks of you? After doing this, how would you describe your perception of your heavenly Father? Is He…

- ◆ Distant?
- ◆ Angry?
- ◆ Indifferent?
- ◆ Disappointed?
- ◆ Absent?
- ◆ Loving you conditionally (only because of Jesus)?
- ◆ Too holy to approach?
    …or can you see Him smiling at you, with a heart full of unconditional love and affection for you?

I have found that people's honest response to this question varies greatly, but very few see Him smiling over them. If you have a negative or neutral view of the Father, don't worry. That's pretty common in today's fatherless culture, and that includes the fatherless religious culture we've inherited. More on that point as we go.

My personal view for the first 25 years of my Christian life was that my heavenly Father was mostly absent. I loved Jesus, talked to Jesus, worshiped Jesus, had encounters with Jesus…but my heavenly Father was not much more than the title I used to begin my prayers. I had no direct relationship with this Father. I did not feel His warm embrace and affirming affections. I lived and thought like a Spirit-filled Christian orphan. This is sad because I found out later that it's precisely why Jesus came, so I could not only meet this Father but have an ongoing, intimate relationship with Him. After all, we are called to be sons and daughters, which means we should know our heavenly Father! Right?

Eventually, through these many encounters with God as my Father, my relationship with this transcendent God of the Universe went from distant, disconnected, and unsearchable, to intimate, full of joy, and abounding in love.

While I certainly have not arrived and still carry residual wounds that hinder my life in Him, at least I know that my ship has left the shore! I've taken passage on my Father's holy cruise liner, sailing His vast ocean of love, and I now know that He will get me to my intended destination. I actually believe now that He is faithful to complete this work He's begun in me,[5] and I also know He's most certainly ready to do the same in you.

In this light, let me lay a biblical foundation for experiencing your own Father Shift. Are you ready to take the most wonderful voyage of your life? All aboard!

WHERE *IS* JESUS LEADING US ANYWAY?

Have you ever considered that the main reason Jesus came to earth was not so we could have our sins forgiven? Now, before you throw this book against the wall and shout, "heretic!" let me explain what I mean. While forgiveness of our sins is incredibly important and re-quired before anything else, we must see that this was only a means to a much greater end. What is this greater end?

First, we should ask ourselves, *where was Jesus trying to take us?*

To some place called heaven when we die? To get a mansion on the other side of glory? Actually, Jesus was talking about a place *in Him*. To live on this earth *from* His Father's house. To see this, let's look at what He said in John's gospel account:

> *I am the way, and the truth, and the life; no one comes* **to the Father** *but through Me. (John 14:6)*

Of course, we all read that Jesus is the only way to the Father and nod our heads, but in our minds we think *"Jesus is only the way to heaven."* At least that's the way I understood it for most of my Christian life. And when I looked around and listened to other believers I knew, they understood it pretty much the same way. More importantly, we lived that way.

My friend, Jonathan Claussen[6] said something very profound when he was speaking at our church recently. He said the following:

> Jesus is the Door and the Way, that is true...but the Door and Way to what? The Church today has been dancing at the door, but Jesus is standing there saying, 'Come in!' We need to go through the Door because that's where the Fa-ther's kingdom is.

This described my worship before I encountered the Father's love for myself—dancing at the Door with Jesus but never actually going in. It's easy to stop and admire Jesus at the door, and that would be a glo-rious life of worship. I don't want to minimize that in any way. But a door leads somewhere. So the question remains...are we going to go *through* the Door where this life Jesus was talking about is waiting for us?

AN ORPHAN'S VIEW OF FATHER'S HOUSE

Orphans are all about finding a warm place to eat and sleep but they don't understand having a home where they're loved and affirmed in a family relationship. They don't understand what it means to *belong*.

Likewise, spiritual orphans want to go to heaven, but they act like they don't care who's there as long as they don't get thrown out in the cold (hell). They know nothing about this invitation into a life with a Father called Love.

Even as born-again Christians, many are living as though presently separated from Him and trusting they'll go to the right place when they go to "meet their Maker," as if God is *outside of them now*. As if they're not seated in heaven with Him right now.[7]

> *Are we going to go through the Door where this life Jesus was talking about is waiting for us?*

We may even think God's generally not happy with us until we get our act together. So, contrary to Jesus' provision to bring us to His Father, we keep our distance.

The truth is, Jesus came into our orphaned world and introduced His Father to us in order to show us how to live in His Father's house. He did this so we could be reunited with Him, right now and forever, no longer orphans but sons and daughters. He told us He would do this by sending the Holy Spirit so that we could live *just like He did* when He walked the earth—abiding in our Father's house and "proving" to this orphan world that our Papa's purpose for them is *good and acceptable and perfect*.[8]

Beloved of God, this world has no mental grid for the Father's love, and the only way they're going to know it is to see it through our lives.[9] And this gets us to the ultimate reason *why* Jesus came.

WHAT WOULD JESUS *ACTUALLY* DO?

Jesus' last discourse in the Gospel of John starts in John 13:31 and goes to the end of chapter seventeen. We must read this as one message with one purpose. And that purpose is to show us how to live *inside* the Father's love, to live like Jesus lived inside His Father's love.

Thomas had asked Jesus where He was going and how can we know the way (14:5). Jesus spends the rest of chapters 14 through 17 answering Thomas' question. To miss this point is to miss everything Jesus is trying to teach us here. Here is a brief synopsis of this common theme running throughout the discourse.

The discourse bookends, front and back, with love (John 13:34-35; 17:21-26). According to Jesus, this is the way the world will know Him—not by our brilliant apologetics, our persuasive oratory, our flawless doctrine, or even our holy, sinless lives. No, it will be by our love *for one another*. This kind of love only comes from first receiving His love by abiding in the Father's love for Jesus. From here, we can summarize this discourse in the following subsections.

John 13:31-38: Jesus tells His disciples that He's leaving and that they cannot follow Him now. Peter responds like all macho spiritual orphans do, that He would die for Jesus. Of course, we know what happened. Peter denies three times that he is a follower of Jesus! Nonetheless, Jesus tells them they will follow Him afterward (13:36). We should be asking, *after what*? This "after what?" is what the rest of the discourse is about.

John 14: Jesus tells His disciples that He is going to prepare a dwelling place for them (14:2-3). Traditionally, it has been taught that we will get a mansion in heaven when we die, but this is not the context here. Jesus is talking about when we receive the indwelling Holy Spirit. He said, *"I will come again and receive you to Myself"* (14:3), which, in this context, is not His Second Coming but when the Holy Spirit would be given.[10] The Holy Spirit is often referred to as the "Spirit of Christ" in

Scripture. We also see this same "coming" in verses 16-18, 21, 23 and 28. Therefore, *"in that day"* (14:20) is about the coming of the indwelling Holy Spirit, not the second coming of Christ.

In verse 18, Jesus states that He will not leave us as spiritual orphans. He sets the stage for our life in the Father as He is in the Father (14:6-11). Jesus is our entrance into this Divine Union, for when we see that we have been placed *in* Christ, we will find our lives in the Father's embrace (14:20). It is from *this place* that we will ask whatever we want from Him and do what Jesus did and greater things, all because we have our heavenly Father's heart (14:12-14). But we won't know this automatically; it comes from sojourning in His love, which is what chapter 15 is about.

Traditionally, it has been taught that we will get a mansion in heaven when we die, but this is not the context here.

John 15:1-25: Jesus tells us how we're to live in the Father's embrace the same way that He lived in His Father's embrace. This is how the Father is glorified: by the fruit of the Spirit[11] (15:4-8). Our fruitfulness comes from living in the Father's love for Jesus (15:9), *staying* where we've already been placed, in the heavenly realm with Him in Christ, partnering with Him by faith as a fully affirmed and authorized son or daughter in His Kingdom (15:14-16).

Jesus also talks here about how this orphan world (and orphan-minded Christians) won't understand this life (15:18-25 and 16:1-4). They won't understand that everything revolves around abiding in the Father's love (15:9-10). They will say that other things are just as important. They are more concerned about *doing something for God* than with *being someone in Him*. Metaphorically speaking, this is eating from the Tree of the Knowledge of Good and Evil instead of the Tree of Life.

John 15:26-16:15: Jesus returns to the workings of the indwelling Holy Spirit. Again, this is the context of this whole discourse and the source of our life in Christ—when the Helper comes (15:26). Jesus is again stressing the main point...where is He going? And why? He's going to the Father so that we can receive the Holy Spirit — the Spirit of adoption and sonship.[12]

Another important point here is found in John 16:8-12. The Spirit of Truth will convict the world of their alienation and brokenness due to sin. He's not doing this with condemnation but with conviction. His Spirit is "convincing" the world of who they really are, why they are, and that they were meant to be in communion with the Father's love. They will either respond to this overture of the Father's affections or reject it. But know this: the Spirit of grace is full of love, and it's His goodness and kindness that leads us into repentance.[13]

Furthermore, Jesus gives us the Holy Spirit to reveal everything that the Father has given us through Him (16:12-15). He does this because we have no mental grid for all that we have in Christ at first. In other words, we cannot go outside of our own knowing. Our unrenewed mind cannot comprehend *the fullness that fills God*[14] living in us. The Holy Spirit must give us divine revelation to go beyond our understanding and into His understanding.

John 16:16-33: This is a parenthetic to the main theme. Jesus takes time to comfort His disciples after disclosing that He will no longer be in the world as they have known Him thus far. The world will later know Him through His new creation — the body of Christ — but His disciples don't understand that at this time.[15]

He alludes to the fact that, while they will leave Him when He is betrayed, He is not alone because His Father is always with Him (16:32). And this brings up a very relevant point for us in verse 33. Jesus tells us that we will have trouble in this world, but the secret to overcoming these things is the same secret He lived in — it's found in the Father's embrace.

John 17: There's a lot I could cover in this chapter, but it goes beyond the scope of this book. What we do need to see here is, first, how Jesus defines "eternal life." It's knowing the Father in Christ (17:3). I will look at this more in depth later.

Second, we see in Jesus' prayer the ultimate reason for His incarnation. It was so that we could all be one, together, in Him, as He has been one with His Father (17:21-26). Again, this is how the world will see Jesus…in us, as we are in Him (17:21, 23). *This* is the Father's game plan for evangelism! Our love for one another as we abide in the same fellowship that the Father has had with the Son since before the foundation of the world (17:24).[16]

> *Is this how you've understood this discourse? Have you ever read it through, as one message?*

Is this how you've understood this discourse? Have you ever read it through, as one message? I ask because most Bible commentaries I've read seemed to have missed this whole point. We tend to chop up and compartmentalize it with our favorite refrigerator verses and, thus, miss the proverbial forest for the trees.

We will continue looking at this discourse and what it means to us throughout the book.

WHAT WAS ON THE FATHER'S MIND WHEN HE MADE YOU?

This Father Shift deals with why He made you and why His Eternal Son had to step into time and space and become human in order to accomplish His dream for us.

I mentioned before that forgiveness was not the ultimate purpose for Jesus becoming a man. While forgiveness of sin is extremely important, it's still only the means to a much greater end. You may be asking, what end could possibly be more important than having our sins forgiven? Paul gives us a glimpse into this with the introduction in his letter to the Ephesians. There is so much here but I will just make a couple of points from the following three verses:

*Blessed be the God and Father of our Lord Jesus Christ, who has blessed us with every spiritual blessing in the heavenly places in Christ, just as **He chose us in Him before the foundation of the world**, that we should be holy and without blame before Him in love, having **predestined us to adoption as sons** by Jesus Christ to Himself, according to the good pleasure of His will, to the praise of the glory of His grace, by which He made us accepted in the Beloved. (Eph.1:3-5)*

First, we need to see that we were chosen by the Father *before He created anything*. This wasn't God's Plan B. Second, His purpose, from before the beginning of anything, was to have sons and daughters. But it's even more wonderful than this!

What Paul is trying to tell us is that God had already decided, before Adam sinned, before you and I sinned, that He would expand the Fellowship that He has enjoyed *within* Himself, to include you inside of this Triune Godhead! If your brain doesn't go tilt right now, you still don't get it!

Dr. C. Baxter Kruger said the following about God's eternal purpose in his *Summary of the Trinitarian Vision*:

> The stunning truth is that this Triune God, in amazing and lavish love, **determined to open the circle and share the Trinitarian life with others.** This is the one, eternal and abiding reason for the creation of the world and of human life. There is no other God, no other will of God, no second plan, no hidden agenda for human beings. [17]

Going back to Jesus' final discourse in John's Gospel, Jesus said something profound about this Father shift that's critical. We need to see ourselves in this eternal fellowship between the Father and the Son in the Spirit. This is the whole point of God's redemptive plan.

At that day you will know that I am in My Father, and you in Me, and I in you. (John 14:20)

Again, I ask, at *what day*? It's the day the Holy Spirit was given; it's the day we see ourselves included in this Divine embrace.

ETERNAL LIFE IN THE FATHER'S EMBRACE

Here's a question for you. When Jesus said that He was the only way to the Father, was He being narrow-minded? Was it an *"It's My way or the highway"* kind of thing? While He is the only means of salvation, I don't think that's what He meant here.

Jesus wasn't talking about getting to heaven when you die as much as stating that the only way we could enjoy the same fellowship that He has had with the Father from eternity was by *being placed in Him.*

> *Eternal life means we've entered into God's very own life, which exists outside of space and time.*

When God became a Man, He became the way into this eternal Fellowship. When He ascended to the Father, we ascended to the Father. [18] We were placed *in* Christ, which brought us into this Divine Circle of God. *This* is what is meant by eternal life.

Eternal life cannot just mean going to heaven or living forever because that, alone, doesn't bring us into this Divine Fellowship. Again, the angels live forever in heaven, but they don't have this relationship *within* the Godhead. Eternal life means that we've entered into the *same* life-giving communion with the Father and the Son in the Spirit that they have enjoyed since before the foundation of the world:

> And **this is eternal life, that they may know You**, the only true God, and Jesus Christ whom You have sent. (John 17:3)

Eternal life means we've entered into *God's very own life*, which exists outside of space and time.[19] We can only do this by being placed in Christ. As we've already seen in John 14:20, Jesus said that the Holy Spirit would help us "know" this new heavenly reality on *"that day"* when He would come to live inside of human beings, as He has been

62

in this communion with the Father before time began. This is where we are, whether we know it or not. Jesus is seated at the right hand of the Father, *and we are in Him.*

The early church fathers saw this mystical union with the Father in Christ. Here are just a couple of quotes from them.

Irenaeus (c. 115 - c. 202) said, *"For this is why the Word became man, and the Son of God became the Son of man:* **so that man, by entering into communion with the Word and thus receiving divine sonship,** *might become a son of God."*[20]

Athanasius (c. 296 – 373), a major contributor to the Nicene Creed, wrote the following: *""He became what we are, so that He might make us what He is...."*[21]

These church fathers aren't saying we're God; they're saying that what happened on *"that day"* is that we were brought into an unprecedented communion in Christ in God. Peter called it being *"partakers of the divine nature."*[22] Jesus became God-inhabited flesh, so that we could become God-inhabited flesh, living *from* the place of this eternal fellowship in heaven, expressing the Father's heart, as Jesus did, on the earth. *This is the life the Father has meant for us* — a life filled with the fullness of God and great joy![23]

Beloved, we need to make this shift in our thinking. We must leave behind the religious lies of separation from God and *be embraced* by our heavenly Papa! It's time to run straight into His arms of love! *This* is where you will find your life — abiding in this Divine Fellowship.

Let these words of John's ring deep in your soul as you ponder these things. This is the very heart and soul of the Christian life:

> *That which we have seen and heard we declare to you, that you also may have fellowship with us; and* **truly our fellowship is with the Father and with His Son Jesus Christ.** *And these things we write to you that your joy may be full. (1 John 1:3-5)*

CHAPTER TWO ENDNOTES

---

[1] Collodi, *Adventures of Pinocchio*, chapter 35.

[2] See James 1:17

[3] SOZO ministry is an inner healing and deliverance ministry. For more information, go to http://bethelsozo.com/

[4] Romans 8:15; Galatians 4:6-7

[5] Philippians 1:6

[6] Jonathan Claussen, founder of Family Restoration Project ministry.

[7] See Ephesians 2:6; Philippians 3:20.

[8] See Romans 12:2

[9] See John 14:17, 19, 27, 30-31; 16:3

[10] See Acts 2:1-21, 33

[11] See Galatians 5:22-23

[12] Galatians 4:4-6; Ephesians 1:5

[13] Romans 2:4

[14] See Ephesians 3:19

[15] See 2 Corinthians 5:16-17

[16] See also Ephesians 1:4-12; 1 John 1:1-4

[17] Kruger, *Summary of the Trinitarian Vision*. Retrieved at http://baxterkruger.blogspot.com/2012/09/summary-of-trinitarian-vision.html

[18] See Ephesians 2:4-6; Colossians 3:1-3

[19] The Greek word for life is zōē. This is not our biological life but the absolute fullness of life, which belongs to God.

[20] From *Saint Jerome: Lives of Illustrius Men*. Retrieved at http://faithofthefathersearlychurchfathers.blogspot.com/2005/10/saint-irenaeus-of-lyons.html

[21] Athanasius, *On the Incarnation of the Word*, Section 54:3

[22] See 2 Peter 1:4

[23] See Ephesians 3:19; John 15:11

CHAPTER THREE

DISCIPLE SHIFT

"She looks at herself instead of looking at you, and so doesn't know you. During the two or three little outbursts of passion she has allowed herself in your favor, she has, by a great effort of imagination, seen in you the hero of her dreams, and not yourself as you really are."

– Prince Karasoff [1]

When we first come to God, we don't see Him as He truly is. We see Him as we think He should be.

We're really only looking at an image of ourselves. We see Him as the God of our dreams who has come to rescue us, but not as He really is. Like Narcissus of Greek mythology, our heart is steadfastly fixed on our own reflection that defines everything we do and everything we think God should be in our lives. We are powerless to break this self-absorbed gaze by ourselves. Only Christ can free us from our reflected selves.

It's not that we haven't truly come to Christ in this state, we have. But the only image we can see of Him is according to what we need Him to be for us. This is not intentional on our part; it's the way we've seen everything in our life up to this point.

And God is very kind and patient on His part to meet us here in this place.

This is the same interpretative lens by which we've learned to evaluate all of our relationships. We may dream of finding "true love," which means someone who will be exactly the way we want and expect them to be.

In other words, they should be...*us*.

They should think like we think and respond the way we would respond. And when they're not us, there's a problem.

This reflective lens—let's call it our "acceptable"—is at the bottom of most marital arguments. And when God, or anyone else in our life, deviates from our expectations of what they should or shouldn't be, we respond with a whole host of negative emotions, which then creates varying degrees of anxiety.

Only Christ can free us from our reflected selves.

All of our conversations with God, and with others, are really about us—what we feel, how we are treated and whether or not people accept us.

Because our existential universe revolves around us, we define God and all our other relationships through this narcissistic lens. God is good...*if* He does what we think is the right thing to do. We are at the center of our universe—the star by which God and all our other relationships must orbit.

Some of us are better at hiding these attitudes than others...at least for a while. While most of us begin to realize eventually, at least in small part, that this is a dysfunctional way to live, some more rare, willful, and stubborn souls can actually keep this up their entire empty lives, leaving a trail of relational brokenness in their wake.

Our Disciple Shift, then, is about no longer relating to our own reflection, and calling it God, to beginning to see Him as He really is. It's putting an end to the *transactional arrangement* we think we've made with Him and allowing Him to walk right into the middle of our deepest pain, sadness, and alienation.

It's allowing Him to help us progressively muddle through our darkness and confusion and into His glorious light *already* residing in us.

DISCIPLESHIP IS ABOUT DISCOVERY

I used to think that discipleship was about learning all about God. This amounted to studying my Bible, being a faithful church attender, hearing lots of messages, taking lots of notes, and trying to go about doing what Jesus did. Add to this, consuming lots of books, blogs and podcasts, and, of course, being accountable to someone who will call me on the carpet if I messed up. It was a lot about learning what I shouldn't do anymore, behaving like a "good Christian," and believing that if I practiced these things long enough, I would accumulate enough "truth" and be free.

This is the definition of true biblical repentance. It's not about being sorry about something; it's about becoming someone new.

Not that any of these things are necessarily bad, it's just that they won't transform the soul and make you truly free.

Discipleship is really about *discovery*.

Our transformation is not about our education or what we should stop doing; it's about discovering who we *already* are through an ongoing cooperative process with the Christ who lives in us.

As C. Baxter Kruger often puts it, it's having our mind, our perceptions, and how we respond to things thrown on the potter's wheel to be re-formed and re-shaped.

This is the definition of true biblical repentance. It's not about being sorry about something; *it's about becoming someone new.* We're not trying to imitate Christ as much as incarnate Christ. That is, allowing Christ's incarnation to work mightily in us.

Discipleship is about learning to do what Jesus *actually* did, which was abide in His Father's embrace.

Once we understand this process, we will begin to actually trust God instead of trusting in ourselves and our own opinion of what's best and hoping He will come through for us.

WHAT ARE WE BEING FREED FROM?

Jesus gave us simple and powerful keys to walking in freedom. Here's how the Message Bible relates what He said about it:

If you stick with this, living out what I tell you, you are my disciples for sure. Then you will experience for yourselves the truth, and the truth will free you. (John 8:31-32 MSG)

We read verses like John 8:31-32 and all nod our heads in agreement. Yes, amen, the truth will make you free. Hallelujah!

Perhaps we should be asking the question, *free us from what*?

You might be tempted to blurt out, sin...free us from sin! Yes, of course, but sin is just a behavioral symptom of something much deeper and more hidden from us. And it is God's good pleasure to help us see it, although it may not feel like our good pleasure at the time. It may even feel like the opposite of good pleasure. Nonetheless, it's good for us if we will just *"stick with this."*

Sin is just a behavioral symptom of something much deeper and more hidden from us.

God will work with us like a good father does his son, the goal being that we will begin to think like He thinks and love like He loves as we grow up into children who have our Father's eyes. And part of that process certainly does concern our sin issues, but only as it helps us to come to a place where sin is no longer seen as a forbidden fruit but more like arsenic to our souls. But even this insight does not touch how He transforms us.

The truth is, we are *already* complete in Him, even at the start of the process.[2] We just don't know what that looks like yet.

Real transformation only *begins* when we allow God to shatter the image of Him that we've made for ourselves, one that's in our own likeness, so we can finally see our true image in *His* likeness.

The freedom Jesus gives also means the end of our trying to live our own life for Him and the beginning of learning how to *have Him live His life in us.* This shift will profoundly affect all our relationships. We're no longer making others jump through our hoops and conform to our expectations because we are now letting them be who they truly are around us.

Experiencing the truth is quite different than reading the Bible and accumulating head knowledge. It's found in *revelation knowledge*. This knowledge must first be revealed in the deepest part of us.

Let me be clear. We *should* read the Bible, but understand that only what is *revealed* to us belongs to us.[3] This also means that we can be talked out of whatever we don't receive by way of revelation.

THE DECORATOR IS HERE!

The problem we have with all of this is that God doesn't usually answer our prayers for change the way we expect or when we expect. Maureen has a great analogy for this process. She will just say, *"The Decorator is here!"* Here's how she puts it.

Say you hate your house. It's old, outdated, and ugly! You want a complete overhaul. One day you happen to meet a world renowned interior decorator and you beg him to come and redo your entire house. He agrees to renovate your home, but explains that he won't be able to do it right away. You agree and go on about your business for several weeks, anxiously awaiting the decorator, and wondering what's taking so long for him to come.

Then, one day, you come home to find that your place is all torn apart, people are stripping floors, peeling off wallpaper, tearing out cabinets and even knocking down walls. It's a mess! Knowing that it's going to be uncomfortable to live with for a while, would you get angry with them and tell them to stop? No, you would rejoice, shouting, *the decorator is here!* You would be excited that the long anticipated renovation had finally begun, knowing that it will be better than you could have ever hoped when it is done.

Likewise, when God answers your prayers and first comes to renovate *you*, it might not be how or when you expected Him to do it. Furthermore, He may have to tear down a few things. They may be things you were comfortable with, things you weren't ready to get rid of. It all may look like a mess at first, even worse than before you started the process with God. But instead of getting angry at Him for making such a mess of your life, realize it's really the answer to your prayers and shout, *"The Decorator is here!"* knowing that when He finishes the upgrade, it will be most glorious because He's making something quite beautiful.

THE MUDDLE IN THE MIDDLE

One part that we don't like about this whole process is what I call the "muddle in the middle." We like the *idea* of transformation, we love the feeling of a fresh start and a new beginning. We long for the end result of true freedom. We even like the idea that we are willing to humble ourselves and submit to God's working. But we usually don't want to go through what's lurking deep inside of us to get there.

We will make every excuse; even create personal doctrines, to avoid it. We would rather jump right to the end and live in a freedom of our own imaginations. We may tell ourselves that if we will just believe, there will be no need for process.

We prefer that our circumstances would change instead of having to change what's inside of us.

This is because, when you're in this process, it may look and feel like you're in hell, and we wish God would just be our magic fixer instead. But God doesn't magically fix us; He works things *in* us, and this can be a painful process. We don't really want to see this truth, so it's often a very messy affair.

This is why you must believe by faith at the outset that God is good and that everything He does is good, even if you're tempted to question His intentions at the time. It's important that we make this transition from living circumstantially to living by faith.

You must also accept full responsibility for your own actions. Remember that everything you do is completely within your own power, whether you believe this or not. You cannot blame your spouse, your parents, your family, friends, boss, or church for *any* action that *you* have taken. You are 100 percent in control of every choice you make and how you respond to other people in any circumstance you may face.

I heard Paul Manwaring[4] say this on a video conference call one time, *"How you respond to something is more important than the something."* This point alone can free you up from of lot of pain and deception, not to mention greatly shortening the process if you will embrace it in your life.

Be aware that you will certainly be tempted to leave this discipleship process during the "muddle in the middle" and go back to the self-imaged world you're comfortable with—one that you still think is protecting you. It probably is protecting you from whatever has hurt you by erecting a relational wall around your heart, but that wall works both ways. It's also keeping out the only One who can transform your soul and bring real freedom.

In order to come to this place of freedom, we all must reach a point in our life when we stop making everything about us. And God is very happy to help us with that transition.

REACHING A MID-LIFE CRISIS IN CHRIST

While what I've called my "glorious crash" in chapter one can happen in many different ways and seasons in our life, I've found that it often happens in our 30 or 40-somethings. Perhaps you've been married for ten or more years. You have growing children and a steady job. Your life feels like you're in the middle of a whirlwind, going from one busy thing to the next.

This transactional construct that you've created with God cannot hold together indefinitely under all this pressure. And He certainly isn't going to help you hold it together. His plan is to let it all come crashing down. Not that He's mean, and He's certainly not trying to punish you, but like with Dickens' Scrooge in the famous Christmas tale, He's going to Holy Haunt you for your own welfare, or should I say, your reclamation.

> *This transactional construct that you've created with God cannot hold together indefinitely*

When I told you that my life was falling apart in my story in chapter one, I was telling you about the beginning of this process for me. I will elaborate more on what I already shared in order to show you what it looked like for me.

My crisis point came when I was in my mid-40s. I had been married for 20 years and our three sons were teenagers at the time. I was an executive director for a very successful business and a leader in our church. But my view of my life in Christ was much like what I mentioned—transactional, formula and principle-based—liking the idea of intimacy with God but keeping Him at a safe distance. I was still very much a spiritual orphan in my thinking, although I didn't know it at the time. My view of the Christian life looked like everybody else's I knew.

I faithfully attended church services, I tithed and gave far above and beyond to those in need. I read my Bible and led Bible studies. I believed in and learned to operate in the gifts of the Spirit. I went to conferences and got excited about the "new thing" God was doing like everyone else. I did everything you're *supposed* to do to have a successful life in Christ. I bought into the "American Dream" version of evangelical Christianity—not so much because of what I was actually taught as much as what I embraced in my culture.

This transactional construct I had created worked satisfactorily …for about 20 years. But when my circumstances began to change for the worse, my view of God began to change for the worse. My roller-coaster marriage was getting more disconnected and distant, the business I was involved in was suddenly failing, and "church stuff" was increasingly more irritating to me.

And all through this spiritual and emotional tailspin, *I kept following the formula*—going to church, praying, tithing, giving, serving, and searching out prophetic words that would assure me that God would come through for me. I kept thinking, *surely God would keep up His end of the bargain.* But eventually we want off the roller-coaster. And I did.

A LOVING GOD IN THE HANDS OF AN ANGRY CHRISTIAN

My pastor at the time all this was happening used to say, *"When you're being squeezed, what's really on the inside of you will come out."* And what was really inside of me was pouring out in bucket loads. But remember when I said that discipleship is about discovery? I was about to discover something very deep and painful *in* me. God was using my own foolishness to reveal something that I was willfully ignorant of until this time.

For about a year before my crash, I was steadily growing angrier at God for not answering my prayers and for *letting all this happen.*

After all, I had been keeping my end of the bargain, but He wasn't keeping His.

I discovered something else here. Whenever we get angry at God, it clearly reveals that our love is self-focused and conditional, even though His love is neither.

I still attended church regularly because of my responsibilities, but my heart was not in it. Eventually, I got to the point where I refused to pray to God at all (remember, I'm a church leader)! My wife and I were barely talking to each other, and I was totally absorbed in trying to keep my business going. I still wasn't willing to go through the process.

In this horrid state, I started to pursue what I thought my heart wanted. That is, doing what I did before I came to Christ. I wanted to go back to before I met my wife and, according to my thinking at the time, before all these troubles began. I got back together with some old friends from the band I used to play with.

> But eventually we want off the roller-coaster. And I did.

We started playing again and I started drinking again. At first, it was just a little bit here and there, but it began to consume more and more of my life. Eventually, I started entertaining the idea of an affair with another woman I met at one of the places where we played. Mercifully, this never fully materialized, but it did provoke the crash, as I mentioned before, which started with the note from my wife saying that she was leaving me for good.

As I was to realize later, God *was* keeping His end of the bargain. But He's not me, so He faithfully let all these illusions about who I thought He was, what I thought my life was supposed to be about, and what I thought would make me happy, all crash and burn.

THE DEATH OF MY TRANSACTIONAL GOD

What came crashing down was this transactional arrangement I thought I had with God. It went like this. If I tithed, prayed the right prayers, studied my Bible, served and did good things, my life would go better. My theology was much like Job's comforters. I prayed like

Job, too. I made sure all the bases were covered in my prayer lists.

You can imagine what happened when my life kept getting worse the more I prayed, tithed, studied and did good things. I got angry at God. After all, He wasn't coming through on my marriage, my business, and my life in general.

What I discovered later is that God didn't want all my "bull and goat" offering prayers and religious acts of service. *He wanted me.* And He wanted me to want Him. I was still the reluctant lover who would not return His overtures of affection. How could I love Him as He was when I only saw my own reflection?

As I mentioned before, this is when God asked me what I wanted to do—leave Him and my mess behind, for what certainly looked like freedom...or walk with Him in the middle of my mess, which seemed like hell to me. I answered, to my amazement, that I wanted Him even if I lost everything else (which I thought I certainly would at the time). I still see this unexpected response as one of most amazing wonders of God's grace working in my life.

> *God didn't want all my "bull and goat" offering prayers and religious acts of service. He wanted me.*

Little did I know at the time, I was about to leave the broken, orphan-hearted veneer I called Christianity, for the rich and vibrant life of Christ! And this life actually works!

It was at this moment when true discipleship with the Word of Life *began* for me. This, after being a so-called Bible-believing, Spirit-filled Charismatic Christian for 23 years, including being an associate pastor in Illinois and a leader in my current church for ten of those years!

One last thing here before we move on. You don't have to have your life fall apart and get angry at God in order to enter this process with Him. You could just learn from other people's failures like mine, and you could cooperate fully with God at the beginning.

But one thing is for certain. *Every person will need to go through this process.* And most of us don't go through it well. At least, at first. Sadly, many never get through it and are left with the wreckage of personal brokenness, along with the brokenness of their marriages and children, as well as with their church families and other relationships.

But when we allow ourselves to go all the way through this process, we will find the real God and then our real selves in Him.

DECIDING TO DO WHATEVER IT TAKES...REALLY

At this point, I feel a little bit like Morpheus from the first Matrix[5] movie. Before we go further, there's one thing you will need to do.

You will need to make a *decision.* And that decision is either do nothing different and stay on the same religious merry-go-round (the blue pill), or commit to doing *whatever* it takes to go through the process (the red pill). With the "red pill," you stay in Kingdom Wonderland and will see just how far Jesus will take you down the rabbit hole of your soul.

The only thing that complicates our life is still having something to protect.

I would say that you need to surrender everything, but you may be thinking you already did that. And that may be true...at least as far as you know at this point. But I want to encourage you. When you finally do this, your life will immediately get much simpler (not necessarily easier).

The only thing that complicates our life is still having something to protect. This doesn't necessarily mean that God wants to take everything away from you. He wants to take the *care* of everything away from you. His promise is that when you do this, you will have whatever you need, although it may not be what you first thought you needed.

I love the way the Message Bible gives Jesus' encouragement...

If God gives such attention to the appearance of wildflowers—most of which are never even seen—don't you think he'll attend to you, take pride in you, do his best for you? What I'm trying to do here is to get you to relax, to not be so preoccupied with getting, so you can respond to God's giving. People who don't know God and the way he works fuss over these things, but you know both God and how he works. Steep your life in God-reality, God-initiative, God-provisions. Don't worry about missing out. You'll find all your everyday human concerns will be met. (Matt.6:31-33 MSG)

Okay, if you're ready, it's time we looked at the process.

LEAVING THE MYTHICAL GOD OF OUR OWN REFLECTION

Understand that the beginning of this freedom in Christ you're looking for comes with the realization that, as much as you want to think otherwise, you didn't initially come to Him because you wanted *His* life. You came for a whole host of other reasons.

Maybe you wanted to feel better about yourself, escape hell and go to heaven, or maybe you wanted to be raptured before the Great Tribulation, or perhaps have Him fix the mess you were in. Maybe it was because you liked the worship music and how it made you feel. Maybe it's just because you were raised that way.

Most of those reasons aren't necessarily bad ones, they're just not why Jesus saved us. And because Jesus actually does love you as much as the Father loves Him, as soon as you say yes to Him, He takes that as permission to take the wrecking ball to this faulty construct.

I think that God actually enjoys destroying these illusions we have about our life in Him. But not because He's mean or sadistic. He's trying to free us from our invisible prison. Our problem is that we often develop Stockholm syndrome[6] with our former captors, even if they are religious in nature.

Israel was afflicted the same way after their exodus from Egypt. God delivered them out of Egypt, but they still needed Egypt delivered out of them. Most of them didn't make it because they would not co-operate with the process. The writer of Hebrews tells us that they failed because they didn't believe the promises, never entering into this "rest" of God. This rest means the end of our working *for* God and the beginning of letting Him work *in* us. It means letting Him live His life in us.

...as soon as you say yes to Him, He takes that as permission to take the wrecking ball to this faulty construct.

God does this work by giving us the Holy Spirit to reveal the truth behind what's going on in our heart. This is the "word of God" *revealed* to us that we've already discussed in John 8:31-32.

Here it is in Hebrews:

> *For the word of God is living and powerful, and sharper than any two-edged sword, piercing even to the division of soul and spirit, and of joints and marrow, and is a discerner of the thoughts and intents of the heart. (Heb.4:12)*

We see here that the Holy Spirit is able to penetrate into our soul life, which is the only life we've ever known to this point.

THE SOUL LIFE AND SPIRIT LIFE

This soul life rules our perception and response to everything we experience. It's how we think things are. To use my Morpheus analogy, it's the world that's been pulled over our eyes. It's called the natural mind, or flesh, in Scripture. It feeds, if you will, from the Tree of the Knowledge of Good and Evil. It's the way we've learned to reason and respond to life on our own, apart from God. It's living circumstantially rather than living by faith.

The Holy Spirit's mission is to get our human spirit, which is in perfect union with Christ in heaven, to lead our circumstantially-driven soul in a completely new way of thinking—what the Bible calls "the mind of Christ."[7] The problem is, we don't actually trust God at all yet. We like to think we do, but we're still keeping Him at the safe distance.

This discovery process, called discipleship, requires bare-naked honest vulnerability, letting Him look under our hood, so to speak, while we would rather have Him look under everybody else's hood.

This life of Jesus that we've been called into *requires* faith. And faith is believing in something you *don't* see or perceive with your natural senses. I will devote a whole chapter on that.

The point here is, we must take courage and trust that real and permanent freedom *only* comes from our learning to let Him touch our deepest darkness. Even atheists can fill their heads with biblical facts, but that doesn't make them a disciple of Jesus any more than loading those facts into a computer would make it a human being.

We are the participants, and everything going on inside of us is fair game.

No, we must leave the safe transactional relationship we think we've made with God and enter into a cooperative process with Him called intimacy. It's been said that intimacy means "in-to-me-you-see." That's a very good definition. We can't do this from a safe distance as spectators, and no one else can do it for us. We are the participants, and everything going on inside of us is fair game. As we allow God to *"discern the thoughts and intents of our heart,"* He uses the soul-piercing sword of His Living Word to shatter the image of the religious god we've made that looks like us. From there, all our other idols will begin to come crashing down.

There's another equally damaging myth that must be shattered at this stage of discovery. It's believing that we "won't have a life" anymore—no fun, no joy, nothing but bowing and scraping and navel-gazing before this mythical religious deity we've created in our mind.

Nothing could be further from the truth! Really. He has something far better in mind for you. He's about to make you come to life for the very first time by showing you how to live *His* wide-open spacious life, a life filled with His joy! And when we allow Him to do this, something wonderful happens: we become free in a totally unexpected way.

I want to give you hope, dear one of God. As Jesus promised, if you *"stick with this"* you will be free.

THE PROCESS OF KNOWING TRUTH

When Jesus was talking about knowing the truth, He was talking about Himself.[8] Truth is a Person. He was talking about an experiential knowing, not an academic one. Without this experiential knowing, we will certainly make a god in our own image and create doctrines based on our own human intellectual limitations. While the Word of God is inspired, it's not inspired to *us* until the Holy Spirit reveals it to us.

All our analytical study tools to dissect Scripture, while helpful, won't necessarily bring us to the Truth. The only way we can get out of our religious mental box is by the Holy Spirit revealing the mind of Christ to us. Let's look at what Paul said about it:

> But as it is written: "Eye has not seen, nor ear heard, nor have entered into the heart of man the things which God has prepared for those who love Him." **But God has revealed them to us through His Spirit.** For the Spirit searches all things, **yes, the deep things of God.** For what man knows the things of a man except the spirit of the man which is in him? **Even so no one knows the things of God except the Spirit of God.** Now we have received, not the spirit of the world, but the Spirit who is from God, **that we might know the things that have been freely given to us by God.** These things we also speak, **not in words which man's wisdom teaches but which the Holy Spirit teaches,** comparing spiritual things with spiritual. **But the natural man does not receive the things of the Spirit of God,** for they are foolishness to him; **nor can**

> *he know them, because **they are spiritually discerned.**
> But he who is spiritual judges all things, yet he himself is
> rightly judged by no one. For "who has known the mind of
> the Lord that he may instruct Him?" **But we have the
> mind of Christ.** (1 Cor. 2:9-16)*

Paul masterfully begins by quoting an Old Covenant truth to show us the New Covenant upgrade. Before we had the indwelling Holy Spirit, we had *no way* of knowing God's thoughts and intents for us.

Traditionally, verse nine is used out of its context in order to sentimentalize about all the things God has prepared for us when we get to heaven. This is unfortunate because it isn't at all what Paul is saying here. There's a *"But God…"* right after this favorite refrigerator verse.

"But God…" means that He has changed something, so we need to pay attention to what comes next.

Paul's whole point is that *now* we *can* know all these things! We have the greatest search engine in the world living right inside of us—the Holy Spirit! He searches out the *deepest things* of God and reveals them *to us.* But we can only learn them by *spiritual* discernment. Another way of saying this is that we will never academically study our way into this without spiritual revelation. We have to get out of our head and into His.

So let's apply this understanding to the discipleship process we've been looking at here.

We come to Christ not knowing what we don't know. In other words, we have no mental grid to be able to think outside of our own head. And even if we could, we probably wouldn't believe it. We would dismiss it because it can't be that simple. Or worse, we *think* we already know it (a symptom of head-knowledge Christianity).

As far as our freedom goes, to the degree we allow Jesus to shine His light into our darkness—remove barriers, wrong thinking, woundedness, abandonment, rejection, self-pity, fears—is the same degree we will begin to experience real freedom.

We will successfully navigate this seemingly vast ocean that lies outside our mental grid by using the compass of faith in God's promises—knowing that *all* the promises of God are *in Him*, yes, and *in Him*, amen, to the glory of God *through* us."[9]

It's believing that He truly works everything for our good because of love and because we believe Him when He says that He has predestined us to be conformed into the image of His Son.[10]

It's the Holy Spirit's work in us that progressively helps us bridge the gap between *who* we are in Christ and *where* we are in our current experience. Again, the Message Bible helps us see how Jesus explains this process:

> *I still have many things to tell you,* **but you can't handle them now.** *But when the Friend comes, the Spirit of the Truth,* **he will take you by the hand and guide you into all the truth there is.** *He won't draw attention to himself, but will make sense out of what is about to happen and, indeed, out of all that I have done and said. He will honor me;* **he will take from me and deliver it to you. Everything the Father has is also mine.** *That is why I've said, 'He takes from me and delivers to you.' (John 16:12-15 MSG)*

There are three things we need to see here.

First, Jesus is saying that our understanding of truth is an *ongoing* process. This doesn't mean we don't already have everything we will ever have in Christ. It means we have no mental grid for all of it yet. So while God's Word never changes, our understanding *must* change and grow, both at a personal level and as the corporate body of Christ.

Truth is objective, but our understanding is often subjective.

True humility requires the willingness to change and *remain* teachable. The Pharisees were rigid in their theological conclusions, and they crucified their long-awaited Messiah. Rigid is not good when it comes to understanding God and growing up into Christ.[11]

Second, Truth is a person—Jesus Christ—which means that Truth is *relational*.

This Truth is living and active in us. And when we stop organically living and growing in Truth, we start dying in our freedom. So, living in the revelation of what we understood about God and ourselves 20 years ago is not acceptable for us today. Jesus Himself spent 18 years in hiddenness, walking in a living relationship process with His heavenly Father, learning how to be a Son with His Father's eyes, growing *"in wisdom and stature, and in favor with God and men."*[12]

Third, we should see that the purpose of the Holy Spirit is to reveal *everything* to us that the Father has given His Son…*"Everything the Father has is also mine. That is why I've said, 'He takes from me and delivers to you.'"*

Why does He do this? Because God is not simply giving us information about Himself, He is giving us *Himself*. Therefore, everything that belongs to Him belongs to us because we have been placed in Him.

At this point I should briefly talk about the place of teachers under this process with the Holy Spirit.

WHO IS TEACHING YOU?

You might ask, if this process is between me and the Holy Spirit, why do I need human teachers or leaders? The first obvious answer is that we each only *"see in part and know in part."*[13] This is the whole point of the five-fold gifts mentioned in Ephesians 4:11-16, to help us *"grow up into Christ."*

But how do we actually get taught? And what is "good teaching?" First, here's what John said about it:

> But the anointing which you have received from Him
> abides in you, and you do not need that anyone teach you;
> but as the same anointing teaches you concerning all

things, and is true, and is not a lie, and just as it has taught you, you will abide in Him. (1 John 2:27)

So how does this verse square with the fact that God gave us teachers to equip us for the work of ministry? It's simply this. When you hear something that has spiritual life to it, your human spirit will confirm it. For instance when someone comes up to me and says that I gave a good teaching, what they're actually saying is that the Holy Spirit was confirming in their heart what I was saying with words. Now, they might not have heard these things before, but when they heard it something came alive in them with an "Amen" in their spirit.

On this note, one of the saddest things in the body of Christ today is a believer's unwillingness to trust the Holy Spirit living in them.

What happens then is, whenever they hear something that may sound different than what they're used to hearing, they will go on the internet, read blogs, watch videos, or they will ask their pastor what he or she thinks...they will do everything but actually ask the Holy Spirit what He thinks! They risk being talked out of something the Holy Spirit wanted to reveal to them that would bring them greater freedom.

Not that asking other people is bad; we should ask, especially when we're still learning how to discern His voice. But our final confirmation should come from the Holy Spirit, not necessarily what the current popular preachers are saying. You have the same Holy Spirit living in you that the best teachers on the earth have. You can trust Him. And good teachers should be equipping you to be able to discern spiritual things from God's Word.

LOOKING IN THE RIGHT MIRROR

What do you normally see when you look in a mirror? Right, you see yourself. We've already talked about how the wrong reflection can keep us from knowing the real God or knowing ourselves and others rightly.

Now, let's look at the right reflection:

Nevertheless when one turns to the Lord, the veil is taken away. Now the Lord is the Spirit; and **where the Spirit of the Lord is, there is liberty**. *But we all, with unveiled face, beholding* **as in a mirror** *the glory of the Lord,* **are being transformed into the same image from glory to glory**, *just as* **by the Spirit** *of the Lord. (2 Cor. 3:16-18)*

Three things to see here.

First, whenever the Spirit is revealing truth to us, there is true liberty. The degree to which we see this truth and embrace it is the degree to which we will walk in freedom in that area of our lives.

Second, we are "beholding" ourselves *in Christ,* who has unveiled our faces to show who we really are. When we finally see God as He really is, we finally see our own true reflection of what God says about us as the Spirit reveals it to us. We move from self-centered love to God-centered love and from self-absorbed identity to our Christ-centered identity. This is the reflection we are to dwell on continually. Christ in us the hope of glory!

Finally, it is the Holy Spirit who is doing this. He is the "mirror," progressively transforming us from our deepest darkness into His glorious light. From our life to His life.

Hopefully, I've laid a foundation for this relational process with God for you. Now, I would like to take the rest of the book to discuss the different aspects of our life in Christ and how my perspective has shifted because of this process.

It's time now to take a look at how to see God rightly.

CHAPTER THREE ENDNOTES

[1] Stendhal, *Le Rouge et le Noir*. There is a classic narcissist in the character of Mathilda. Says Prince Korasoff to Julien Sorel, the protagonist, with respect to his beloved girl (Page 401, 1953 Penguin Edition, trans. Margaret R.B. Shaw). Retrieved at http://en.wikipedia.org/wiki/Narcissus_%28mythology%29

[2] See Colossians 2:10

[3] See Deuteronomy 29:29

[4] Paul Manwaring, author and senior leader at Bethel Church in Redding, CA.

[5] Wachowski Bros., *The Matrix* (1999). If you want to see the Morpheus scene I'm talking about you can go to http://youtu.be/zE7PKRjrid4.

[6] Stockholm syndrome a psychological phenomenon in which hostages express empathy and sympathy and have positive feelings toward their captors, sometimes to the point of defending and identifying with the captors.

[7] See 1 Corinthians 2:16

[8] See John 14:6

[9] 2 Corinthians 1:20

[10] See Romans 8:28-30

[11] See Ephesians 4:13-15

[12] See Luke 2:52

[13] See 1 Corinthians 13:9

CHAPTER FOUR

THEOLOGY SHIFT

"Jesus Christ is perfect theology" – Bill Johnson

When Soviet leader Nikita Khrushchev defiantly declared that his cosmonaut returned from space and had not found God, C.S. Lewis responded, *"Looking for God—or Heaven—by exploring space is like reading or seeing all of Shakespeare's plays in the hope you will find Shakespeare as one of the characters…"* [1]

If we're like Hamlet in one of Shakespeare's plays, how would we know Shakespeare? As Lewis also said, Shakespeare would have to write himself into the play. And indeed, God did this with the incarnation of Christ.

But the truth is much more fantastic than this. To use our analogy, not only has Shakespeare "written himself in" by coming to live in the middle of Hamlet's dark and haunted world, Shakespeare has put Hamlet inside of himself!

I've already referenced him in previous chapters but I want to acknowledge the teaching of Dr. C. Baxter Kruger[2] before we go further. I recommend you read his books and his lecture series to get a scholarly understanding of what I am proposing. It's important that we get this because everything we can know about God comes from the foundation I will attempt to lay out here.

Theology, by definition, is the study of God. And how we know God frames everything else that we will ever understand about life. The question is, *how can we know God*? As Dr. Kruger asks, how can we believe that we are in actual contact with God and not with an echo of our own souls? How are we going to escape our own darkness? To use C.S. Lewis' analogy, how is Hamlet ever going to know his creator when there is an infinite gulf between them?

To use our analogy… Shakespeare has put Hamlet inside of himself!

Since this is not a theology book, I will not exhaustively cover the subject here. I will only cover points relating to shifting our relationship with God from an orphan mindset[3] of separation to one of intimacy as a beloved son or daughter in the Father's embrace. I will also attempt to greatly simplify this understanding for our purposes here.

There are three aspects to the truth of how God has made it possible for us to literally know Him, according to Scripture. The first is that God knows Himself in the Father, Son and Spirit, and has been in communion within Himself from before creation. God shares everything together within this Holy Communion:

> *In the beginning was the Word, and the Word was with God, and the Word was God. (John 1:1)*

The second aspect is that because God knows Himself in the Father, Son and Spirit, we can know God in the person of Jesus Christ. God the Son, the eternal Word, traversed this infinite gulf between Himself and mankind, to dwell among us in human flesh. In other words, Shakespeare wrote himself into Hamlet's world!

> *And the Word became flesh and dwelt among us, and we beheld His glory, the glory as of the only begotten of the Father, full of grace and truth. (John 1:14)*

Scripture also reveals Jesus as the perfect expression of God.[4] Therefore, we can know God's nature and character by looking at Jesus. We don't define God, then look at Jesus; we look at Jesus to define God. *Jesus Christ is the lens through which we see God as He really is.* We will look at that point in greater detail in a moment.

So far, we know that Jesus Christ was with God the Father before creation and that He is the exact representation of God for us. If this was all there was to it, only Jesus knows God and we could only be able to observe Him from the outside looking in. But God doesn't stop here!

The third aspect of this truth that allows us to truly know God is that Jesus sent us His Holy Spirit, and *He* will reveal *everything* about Himself by coming to live *in* us. Here's what Jesus said about the indwelling Holy Spirit:

> *He will glorify Me, for* **He will take of what is Mine and declare it to you.** *All things that the Father has are Mine. Therefore I said that* **He will take of Mine and declare it to you.** *(John 16:14-15)*

But this isn't even the most fantastic thing that God has done here. Not only did Jesus reveal God to us by His life, and send His Holy Spirit to live in us, *He put us inside of Himself!* In other words, not only did Shakespeare come to live in Hamlet's world, he put Hamlet *inside* of Shakespeare!

Do you understand what this means, dear one in Christ? This means that you and I can know God *the same way God knows God!* Look at the following statements of Scripture:

> **At that day** *you will know that* **I am in My Father, and you in Me, and I in you.** *(John 14:20)*

> **I in them, and You in Me;** *that they may be made perfect in one, and that the world may know that You have sent Me, and have loved them as You have loved Me. "Father,* **I desire that they also whom You gave Me may be with Me where I am,** *that they may behold My glory which You*

have given Me; for You loved Me before the foundation of the world. (John 17:23-24)

And **God raised us up with Christ** and **seated us with him** *in the heavenly realms in Christ Jesus" (Eph. 2:6 NIV)*

As we saw in chapter two (Father Shift), *"at that day"* means when we received the indwelling Holy Spirit. For everything in John 14 is about our adoption as sons by our receiving of the Holy Spirit.

Summarizing, we CAN truly know God because:

1. God knows Himself in the Father, Son, and Spirit apart from creation. They share all things in communion within the Godhead.

2. We can know God through Jesus Christ. Anything we say about God, whether in the Old Testament or New Testament, that's different from the nature or character of Jesus is not the true nature or character of God. It's something we've interpreted through our own darkened lens.

3. We can know God through *spiritual intimacy.* Not only does God's Spirit dwell in us and reveals all things given to Jesus, but we have literally been placed into the *same union* (by the indwelling Spirit) that the Father has had with the Son from before creation.

At this juncture, I would like to elaborate on the second and third summary points. I think it's important because, in my view, it's the very center of our theology.

JESUS CHRIST IS PERFECT THEOLOGY

Bill Johnson made this brilliant statement which I believe succinctly sums up everything we can know about God. We find this perfect theology of Love all wrapped up in God as a Father and expressed to us by His Son, Jesus Christ. And Love's continuing mission is for Him, by His Spirit, to be lived out in human beings on the earth.

You may have some questions about this seemingly simplistic conclusion, but before we get to that, here is the scriptural evidence for the premise that Jesus is perfect theology:

> *And He is the radiance of His glory and the **exact representation of His nature**, and upholds all things by the word of His power. (Heb. 1:3 NASB)*

> ***If you had known Me, you would have known My Father also**; from now on you know Him, and have seen Him. (John 14:7)*

What these passages tell us is that Jesus didn't just act like His Father, He was the *exact representation of His nature*. That also means that anything that contradicts how Jesus described His Father in His parables, or how He expressed His heart toward all people by word and deed, is not the true nature of God. What this is also saying to us is that the *only* accurate interpretative lens for understanding God is through the "lens" of Jesus Christ. In other words, you cannot have Jesus acting one way toward sinners and the Father acting in some other way.

If we want to understand God, we start with Jesus Christ, not the Old Testament.

If we want to understand God, we *start* with Jesus Christ, *not* with the Old Testament. This is important because it unravels a lot of ideas we have woven about what we think God is like.

WHAT ABOUT GOD IN THE OLD TESTAMENT?

Of course, this raises an obvious question, and it's an important one because it often causes people to turn away from God. *What about the God of the Old Testament?* After all, He didn't seem to be acting like Jesus or the prodigal son's father at all!

We can all point to passages where God seems to be telling His people to wipe out every man, woman, child, dog and cat, or where He seems to look the other way at the immoral or unethical shenanigans of His own leaders. That doesn't sound much like what we see in Jesus, does it? Well, it doesn't for good reasons that go beyond the scope of this book, but let me unpack one important one here.

To understand this apparent contradiction, we first need to look at something Jesus said that is very profound:

> All things have been handed over to Me by My Father; and **no one knows the Son except the Father; nor does anyone know the Father except the Son**, and anyone to whom the Son wills to reveal Him. (Matt. 11:27 NASB)

Do you realize what Jesus is saying here? He's saying that *no one* actually knew God before Jesus came to earth! Not Adam, not Noah, not Moses, not David. I want this to percolate in your brain for a minute. John tells it this way:

> No one has seen God at any time; the only begotten God who is in the bosom of the Father, He has explained Him." (John 1:18 NASB)

What Jesus and John are both saying is that all throughout history, God's people never actually knew God *as He really was*—that is, until Jesus *"explained Him."* Only Jesus gives us the Divine commentary on the true nature of God. Yes, they had a relationship with God before Jesus' incarnation, but they never saw or understood Him as He truly is, for God could not show His true nature to them.

Since Adam, and through Israel's history, God could only relate to mankind at a level that *they* could comprehend. As David said:

> You prove to be loyal to one who is faithful; you prove to be trustworthy to one who is innocent. You prove to be reliable to one who is blameless, but you prove to be deceptive to one who is perverse. (2 Sam. 22:26-27 NET)

In other words, God revealed Himself to people *according to their own reflection.* As we saw in the last chapter, spiritual orphans only see others, or God, according to how *they* themselves think or act, not as others really are. And we were all spiritual orphans before God came to make His home in us through the indwelling Holy Spirit.

In the Old Testament, we see God dealing with the bloody and violent world of Noah, then bringing Abraham out of his pagan Babylonian roots, progressively walking Israel out of their idolatrous culture—deconstructing the Egyptian gods through the animal sacrifices. He showed Himself violent to the violent, merciful to those who show mercy, and loyal to the faithful. They only saw glimpses of God's true nature all throughout the Old Testament and could only represent Him in Scripture as *they* understood Him.

It wasn't until Jesus came that we could actually know God as He truly is. As a fully affirmed Son, Jesus was the 200-proof, undiluted God of love in human flesh! That point alone should speak volumes to us.

Maybe this illustration will help us here.

Say I'm a father who has a son. When he is two-years old, I will play with him on the floor, join in his imaginary games, my communication with him will be very simplistic. I will say "no" to him often and give him very little freedom. I may even yell at him when he's about to run into the street. He won't understand why, but my motive as a good father is to protect him. To an outside observer, my rules might seem very curt and my relationship very strict.

As my son grows older and develops as a human being, the rules will change and he will have more freedoms. I no longer have to stop him from running in front of a car or touching a hot stove. Finally, when he's an adult, I have no rules for him to follow because he can think for himself and protect himself. He's a totally free person, but he's still my son. In fact, he's taken on some of my nature and acts a lot like I do. The point is, our relationship is totally different than when he was two-years old.

So here's my question. Did I change as a father?

Of course, I didn't change. I was the same father throughout his entire life. My son is the one who changed. Now that he's an adult, he has the ability to understand me as I truly am.

We can see God's relationship with His people this way. Israel was like a small child with our heavenly Father, under the strict tutelage of the Law. We can see "full adulthood" in Jesus, and now in us, as our heavenly Father's sons and daughters who have the indwelling Holy Spirit and who know who we are in Him. God no longer relates to us at all like He did with Israel. Here's how Paul explains this relational progression:

> Even so we, **when we were children**, were in bondage under the elements of the world. **But when the fullness of the time had come**, God sent forth His Son, born of a woman, born under the law, to redeem those who were under the law, **that we might receive the adoption as sons.** (Gal. 4:3-5)

Do you see it yet? God did not change as a Father. We (mankind) grew up. And when we were ready—*when the fullness of time had come*—God became flesh as a firstborn Son, and now we can finally see and understand God as He truly is.

Jesus was upgrading their view of God

This is why Matthew records Jesus telling His followers, *"You have heard it said, but I say...."*[5] His teachings and actions were actually overruling the Old Covenant truth with *greater* truth about God. Jesus was upgrading their view of God to how He really felt about things. In other words, as Jesus told Thomas in John 14:7, *"From now on you know Him, and have seen Him..."*

"From now on" we know God in Jesus Christ. This is why you cannot view God through the "glasses" of the Old Covenant and why you cannot base your relationship with God on Old Covenant truths—especially where they contradict New Covenant truths. Jesus Christ is the beginning and end of all theology.

In the last chapter, we looked at the distortions we have about God in our own soul. Now we will turn our attention to a few distortions and myths that have been taught to us through religion about God.

DO WE HAVE A DR. JEKYLL AND MR. HYDE GOD?

This shift in our theology involves confronting some of the popular theories about God that have made the Father different than Jesus in His nature or intentions toward us. Thankfully, God is raising up inspired teachers today who are helping us deconstruct these deeply held theories and actually get back to a view of God that the early church fathers embraced. I will share some of those breakthroughs here.

While our popular but conflicted modern view of the triune nature of God is no doubt unintended, nonetheless, it creates subtle but very harmful contradictions about God.

Case in point: on July 8, 1741, Jonathan Edwards brilliantly gave a lurid description of an angry deity in his famous sermon to his congregation in Enfield, Connecticut, titled, "Sinners in the Hands of an Angry God." This vivid persona of an angry God is deeply entrenched in our thinking about how our heavenly Father feels about us. I esteem Jonathan Edward's brilliant teachings with high regard in his other works, but I think he was having some "father issues" here! Does God really hate sinners so much that He dangles them like a spider over a fire until we submit?

Let's apply the Jesus test. *Is this how Jesus treated sinners?* Does this sound like His Father who *loves* the world *so much* that He gave what was most valuable to Him—His only begotten Son?

Do we have a meek and compassionate "Dr. Jekyll" Jesus, and an angry and sadistic "Mr. Hyde" Father?

The obvious answer should be "no."

Our view of God as our Father is like a replay of the scene in Dickens' *A Christmas Carol*, where Ebenezer Scrooge's sister Fan acts as the intermediary between him and his harsh, disciplinarian father. See if her words resonate with our popular view of Jesus allegedly placating an angry Father in the following:

> "Father is so much kinder than he used to be, that home's like Heaven. He spoke so gently to me one dear night when I was going to bed, that I was not afraid to ask him once more if you might come home; and he said 'Yes, you should'; and sent me in a coach to bring you." [6]

This view is like asking your mom for something because you don't want to risk having your angry dad blow up again. After all, who wants to go to *"The God that holds you over the Pit of Hell, much as one holds a Spider, or some loathsome Insect, over the Fire, abhors you, and is dreadfully provoked."* [7] Who wants to go to someone who slaughtered His own kid so He could forgive you! It's quite sad how some of us think of our heavenly Father.

Let's apply the Jesus test. Is this how Jesus treated sinners?

Before you dismiss what I'm saying because I'm putting the knife to one of your evangelical "sacred cows," did you know that this "God's wrath needs satisfaction" atonement paradigm began with a man named Anselm in the eleventh century? John Calvin further developed this view of appeasing an angry god in the sixteenth century, with what sounds like some angry child-abusing father who would rather kill us but kills His own son instead!

But the fact is, nobody believed this medieval view of God before then, and the Eastern Orthodox Church has never embraced this view. They see God's justice as *restorative* rather than punitive. God came to *save* sinners because of His love for them. The cross was not satisfying the wrath of an angry God but was a rescue mission from a loving God.

The topic of atonement theories and how we got here is beyond the scope of this book and is a subject I am working on for a future book. I also cover this subject on my blog at http://melwild.wordpress.com.

GOD CAN'T EVEN LOOK AT OUR SIN...REALLY???

This particular myth is insidious in that it locks us out in shame and condemnation by believing one of the devil's favorite lies—that God will have nothing to do with us until we "get our act together." After all, His eyes are too pure to look at our sin, right?

This is classic religious orphan-hearted separation.

You might object by saying, *but doesn't the Bible say exactly that...that He can't even look at our sin?* This belief comes from the way we've interpreted one verse in the Bible. Actually, it's only the first half of a verse! It's found in Habakkuk:

> *You are of purer eyes than to behold evil, **and cannot look on wickedness**. (Hab. 1:13a)*

I've heard this line quoted at least a hundred times, usually in some canned salvation appeal, but did we ever bother to read the rest of the verse and find out the context?

> ***Why do You look on those who deal treacherously**, and hold Your tongue when the wicked devours a person more righteous than he? (Hab. 1:13b)*

Who has the seeing problem here? It wasn't God, it was Habakkuk! He's asking why God is actually looking on when people are doing evil things. In *Habakkuk's* mind, God's eyes are *supposed to be* too pure to even look at such things. Back in verse 3, we see Habakkuk lamenting over the same issue. I will use other translations to bring this out more clearly:

> *Why do you make me see wrongdoing? **And why do you watch wickedness**? (Hab. 1:3 GW)*

> *Why do you make me see such trouble? **How can you stand to look on such wrongdoing**? (Hab. 1:3 GNT)*

Again, who is the one with the perception issues here? Yeah, Habakkuk! Much like Jonah...and us...he was having an issue with God's scandalous grace for people who didn't *deserve* it. Likewise, we are projecting our own issues onto God when we take this verse out of context.

This faulty understanding has created a very conflicted view of the Trinity. We have God the Father who can't even look at sin, yet Jesus—who we believe to be God the Son—accused of being called a drunkard and a friend of sinners![8] And why did they accuse Jesus of such things? Because He *actually* hung out with drunks, prostitutes, and all sorts of evil sinners!

I put this question to you: if Jesus is God as we say He is, then why was He constantly exposing Himself to such wickedness since God supposedly cannot countenance such things? Besides, if Jesus truly was in the Father, and Jesus said He was, wasn't He also dragging His Father into all this evilness?

Let's put one last coffin nail in this myth. Jesus said this about Himself:

> Then Jesus answered and said to them, "Most assuredly, I say to you, the **Son can do nothing of Himself, but what He sees the Father do; for whatever He does**, the Son also does in like manner. For the Father loves the Son, **and shows Him all things that He Himself does**..." (John 5:19-20)

Here's a question for you. *Whose* lead did Jesus say He was following? Was it not the Father showing Him how He should befriend wicked people? How, then, does this statement by Jesus Himself inform us about what our heavenly Father can or cannot look at?

Let me make this perfectly clear. It was the FATHER'S idea for Jesus to look demon-possessed people straight in the eye, touch lepers, heal a heathen Roman soldier's servant, forgive the adulterous woman, engage in conversation with the Samaritan divorcé, embrace greedy Zacchaeus, hang out with the worst of His culture, and pick low-life tax collectors and a traitor to be His closest friends.

Beloved, He's the prodigal's Father who throws a party when religious people demand retribution. He's the one healing the sick, setting the captive free, raising a grieved mother's dead child back to life, doing good to evil people through His Son wherever He goes...THIS IS YOUR FATHER!!!

> *If you had known Me, you would have known My Father also; and from now on you know Him and have seen Him. (John 14:7)*

THE FATHER DID NOT ABANDON JESUS

The Father had to turn away from Jesus at the cross. This popular myth haunts the deepest part of us because it touches our fear of abandonment. Let's face it, if the Father turned away from Jesus in His darkest hour, why wouldn't He turn away from us in our sin?

I can appreciate how having a picture of Jesus being forsaken by everyone, even His own Father, creates heart-felt sentimentalities that make us love Jesus all the more.

However, in a much deeper and darker place in our soul, it also makes us wonder about how good this Father is, who would abandon his own Child...*under any circumstances.*

He's the prodigal's Father who throws a party when religious people demand retribution.

The truth is, the Father *never* abandoned Jesus, not for one moment. He was IN Christ reconciling us to Himself when WE looked away, as we see in the following:

> **God was in Christ** reconciling the world to Himself... (2 Cor. 5:19a NIV)

Where was the Father during the crucifixion? He was IN Christ reconciling us back to Himself. If the Father was in Christ, He was hardly looking away!

Right about now, you may be thinking, what about Jesus crying out on the cross, "*My God, My God, why have You forsaken Me?*"[9] Yes, He was quoting the beginning of Psalm 22, but the real question is, *why* was He quoting it?

We must understand that whenever someone quoted one line of Scripture in Jesus' religious culture, the audience would understand it in the context of the whole passage. The New Testament writers also did this. They didn't turn Scripture into refrigerator-verse platitudes the way we like to do.

> *He was taking our darkness and orphan blindness to the cross so that we would never be separated from Him again.*

Jesus quoted the first line of Psalm 22 to refer to the *whole psalm*, which is a very detailed prophetic dialogue of the crucifixion. But what does it say in the SAME Psalm when we read the rest of it for context?

> *For He has not despised nor abhorred the affliction of the afflicted; **nor has He hidden His face from Him**; but when He cried to Him, He heard. (Psalm 22:24)*

Did you catch that? The psalmist is prophetically declaring that God will *not* hide His face from Jesus, nor will He abhor Him so much that He was deaf to His affliction.

So what was Jesus doing here? He was identifying with *our* feelings of abandonment and separation from God on a human level. He was taking *our* darkness and orphan blindness to the cross so that we would never be separated from Him again. As Isaiah prophesied, WE were the ones who "*esteemed Him stricken, smitten by God, and afflicted.*"[10] It was *our* grief, *our* sorrow that He took upon Himself. It was not His, for He and His Father were always in intimate union, which is critically important for us to see.

Jesus said to His disciples on the night of His betrayal that *they* would all leave Him, yet His Father would *never* leave Him:

> *Indeed the hour is coming, yes, has now come, that you will be scattered, each to his own, and will leave Me alone. And* **yet I am not alone,** *because* **the Father is with Me.** *(John 16:32)*

Next, notice very carefully what Jesus says in John 8:28. He's clearly talking about His crucifixion here:

> *Then Jesus said to them,* **"When you lift up the Son of Man,** *then you will know that I am He, and* **that I do nothing of Myself;** *but as My Father taught Me, I speak these things. And* **He who sent Me is with Me. The Father has not left Me alone,** *for I always do those things that please Him.*

Okay, so what do statements like, *"He who sent me is with Me"* and *"The Father has not left me alone"* usually mean to you? Do you see it yet?

Jesus leaves no doubt here. He did *nothing* of Himself, He was never alone and nothing ever separated Him from His Father, not even the sin of the world.

Your heavenly Father is not an absentee Dad.

Beloved child of God, your heavenly Father is not an absentee Dad. He won't run off on you...*ever.* He never left Jesus in His hour of greatest pain and He will never ever, ever forsake you either!

Let the following emphatic declaration of the Father's commitment to you wash over your soul (brackets and parentheses are in translation):

> *For He [God] Himself has said, I will not in any way fail you nor give you up nor leave you without support. [I will] not, [I will] not, [I will] not in any degree leave you helpless nor forsaken or let [you] down (relax My hold on you)! [Assuredly not!] (Heb. 13:5b AMP)*

IS GOD ANGRY WITH SINNERS EVERY DAY?

I had a daily radio spot a few years back called, "God Moments." The theme was always about the goodness of God, encouraging my listeners to accept the invitation into His loving embrace. On one of the programs, I mentioned that God is not angry at us and that He's like the Prodigal's father who's waiting for us to open our hearts to His love. When I got back to my office there was a message on my phone from an angry woman that went something like this…

"You are deceiving people! The Bible says that God is angry with sinners every day…you need to tell them the truth!"

Click!

Of course, this woman was parroting what many Christians have been taught to believe, and they get this from one solitary verse in the Bible—Psalm 7:11. It's actually from the King James Version as follows:

*God judgeth the righteous, and God is angry **with the wicked** every day.*

Case closed, right? Well, it would be if that's what it actually said in the original language.

You see, the words *"with the wicked"* aren't in the original text. The translators *added* what they thought was meant here. This is a normal practice in translating Scripture and not necessarily bad, but sometimes these *interpretations* can lead to confusion, or just plain wrong ideas about God.

Understand that while the original text of Scripture, in the original language, with the original intent and meaning is inspired by God, the English translation is not necessarily inspired. This is why it's good to have several translations to make sure you're getting the true essence of what God is actually saying rather than one particular highly educated guess on what was meant.

Let's look at this verse in other translations:

*God [is] a righteous judge, and He is **not** angry at all times.
(Young's Literal Translation)*

Wow, that has quite a different spin, doesn't it! This very literal rendering of the original Hebrew text says that God is *not* angry at all times with no mention of the wicked here. Now, how about a more modern rendering:

*God is a fair judge, a God **who is angered by injustice**
every day. (God's Word Translation)*

My own biased interpretative lens (we all have one) would probably prefer this rendering. Again, which one sounds more like the God who *is* love to you? Which one sounds like Jesus?

What actually angers God? It's not sinners or the wicked. *It's injustice.* He is always *for* His kids...and that's you! Like any loving parent, He will do anything to free His children from abuse.

> *God is not
> conflicted... We are
> the ones with the
> conflict here.*

You might respond by saying that people do unjust things, but the New Testament revelation clearly points to Satan and his demonic principalities of darkness as the real perpetrators. God sees His kids as victims of Satan's devices.[11] His heart is to free us from Satan's bondage, not one of perpetual hatred.

Didn't this Father *"so love"* every person who will ever inhabit this world, even those who hate Him, that He gave His Son to release us from the entanglements and toxicities of our bondage and alienation, so that we could be with Him forever?[12]

Jesus did not come to condemn sinners but to free them from their prison. God is not conflicted. He's not loving the world He died for and hating them every day at the same time! *We* are the ones with the conflict here.

Salvation was not a legal transaction made in some heavenly courtroom to satisfy an angry judge, it was a rescue mission planned in the heart of a loving Father.

Hopefully, I've cleared up some major issues that keep us hiding from God in fear. Now, let's look at God at the very core of who He is.

GOD IS RELATIONAL BEFORE ANYTHING ELSE

Another theological shift we need to make is a relational one. We typically make doctrinal agreement more important than relationship. This is also one reason why we have over 33,000 denominations in the body of Christ today! But God expresses Himself in Scripture as a Father who loves a Son in perfect fellowship with Him from eternity. This means that God is first and foremost about relationship and family before anything else.

God IS love[13] which *requires* being in relationship *within Himself.* Love, by definition, must be expressed as an action in the context of relationship. God could not *be* love if there were no other object of that affection within Himself. In other words, if God required something or someone outside of Himself, He could *express* love like we do, but He could not *be* love.

God is love, eternally expressed between the Father, Son and Spirit, apart from His creation, apart from anything outside of Himself. We know this from Jesus' own teaching:

> *Father, I desire that they also whom You gave Me may be with Me where I am, that they may behold My glory which You have given Me; **for You loved Me before the foundation of the world.** (John 17:24)*

You can only truly understand the nature of God's love and goodness within the context of this eternally reciprocating relationship between the Father, Son and Holy Spirit. The early church fathers understood this and fought to preserve this revelation and hammered this out in documents like the Nicene Creed.[14]

FAMILY MATTERS

As I've already stated, because God is a Father, it also means that He is about family. Let me share an encounter I had with Him on this point.

My mother had just barely made it into the second decade of the twenty-first century, dying at the age of 93 on January 2, 2010. She had lived a good, long life and had seen a lot of changes over the decades. The week after her death, I had been poring over old photographs of her side of my family. I even got to read her diary from the early 1930s when she was in high school. All of this was a healing experience for me.

Every human being wants to belong.

At this same time, I happened to be at a place in my Bible reading where the genealogies are listed. You know, the parts we skim through to get to the important stuff. Well, this time the Lord interrupted me in the middle of my skimming with a very clear voice (not audible).

"Why do you think I put all those names in there?"

I had never really thought about it before, so He had my attention. He then told me that these names were in there because *every name was a life that mattered*. These people lived lives that were an integral part of His-story. What the Lord had shown me is how each generation had contributed something to the Messianic family legacy.

You see, sonship is about belonging. God didn't just pop out of the sky without any relationship to the people He came to save. Think about it. Jesus could trace His family tree, unbroken, all the way back to Adam! And every generation contributed something to who He was as the Son of Man, to His human DNA, identifying Him fully with us.

Then I began to think about how important belonging is to us. Even adopted orphans long to know where they came from. We have in us an innate need to be part of something bigger than ourselves. Every human being wants to belong. God answers that deep longing by placing us in His BIG family that exists both in heaven and on the earth.[15]

While doctrine is very important, and our doctrinal agreement would be wonderful, none of this is as important as our union together in Christ. I will talk more about this in the last chapter.

Let this thought sink deeply into your soul. Since God has revealed Himself in Scripture as Father, Son and Spirit, this means there has never been a time when He has *ever* been alone. He has always been Father, Son and Spirit, in perfect love and communion. This is very good news because this also means that *you will never be alone.* You are *always* in this Divine fellowship and family!

This is an absolutely stunning reality that we need to get a hold of. Maybe exploring the following question will help us see it.

WOULD JESUS STILL NEED TO COME IF ADAM NEVER SINNED?

I once asked my congregation and my blog readers this question. I did so to disconnect them from a sin-centered view of Jesus' incarnation. Of course, this question might seem irrelevant since Adam did sin, but entertaining it does highlight a point I think we miss.

Most answered, no. You may too.

Jesus did come to die for our sins. So, yes, forgiveness is critical, but what about *redemption*? To redeem means to recover, to bring into relationship. Reconciliation means to restore relationship.

Here's my point. If Adam had never sinned, he, and we, would've lived forever *with* God, but we would not be placed *in* Him. In other words, we would not have been included *in* this Divine Fellowship.

Without the incarnation of Christ, we would be like the angels, *with* God in heaven, but we would not be *in Christ*. The fact is, in order for humans to be included in this divine fellowship with the Father in

Christ, God must place us in Himself as a human being.

Jesus, by taking on human flesh, healed every part of our damaged condition called sin by fusing His human nature to divinity and carrying it to the cross. Indeed, this is what the early church fathers fought to preserve. Here is a quote from Cappadocian father, Gregory of Nazianzus (329-389 AD):

> For that which He [Christ] has not assumed He has not healed; but that which is united to His Godhead is also saved. If only half Adam fell, then that which Christ assumes and saves may be half also; but if the whole of his nature fell, it must be united to the whole nature of Him that was begotten, and so be saved as a whole.[16]

And this is exactly what He did in Christ! When Jesus died, we died, when He was buried, we were buried. When He rose again, we were raised with Him to newness of life. When Jesus ascended to the right hand of the Father, we ascended with Him.[17]

Think about this. Right now, you're *inside* this Eternal Communion between the Father and the Son by the Spirit because there is a Man in that Fellowship and you were placed inside that Man! This is the ultimate *Sonshift!* And you and I have been included in it. As Dr. Kruger puts it, *"The great dance of unchained communion and intimacy, fired by passionate, self-giving and other-centered love, and mutual delight."*[18]

RELATIONAL THEOLOGY IS HEART THEOLOGY

If God is primarily relational, then we are talking more about issues of the heart than the head. And this brings up a problem in understanding our traditional systematic theology.

Why do I say this? Well, do *you* read systematic theology? I rest my case. And if you actually do happen to read systematic theology, you're in the minority. Most people don't because it usually reads like the owner's manual to the space shuttle. There are absolutely brilliant theologians who can disseminate deep truths about God in these ponderous tomes. The only trouble is, they're trying to reach our head instead of our heart.

This Theology Shift, then, is moving away from filling our heads with information *about* God, to enlarging our hearts *in* God. It's the difference between knowing how to accumulate more facts about God and learning how to *experience more of Him.*

> *It's puzzling to me that we spend so much time pounding information about God into people's heads and so little time teaching them how to open their hearts to Him.*

It's like the difference between knowing all the facts about my wife and actually experientially *knowing* her. Hopefully, you get my point. Of course, with God, this intimacy is a relational union, not a sexual one. The point is that it's *that* intimate—full of passion, infinite joy and pleasure.[19]

It's puzzling to me that we spend so much time pounding information about God into people's heads and so little time teaching them how to open their hearts to Him.

Let me give you an illustration of what I mean.

If I were to ask you to point to yourself, where would you point? (Point to yourself right now).

Why did you point to your heart and not your head?

The reason we don't point to our head is because *who we are comes from the heart.* When I say "heart," I mean the center of our affections. People working in the sales professions know that buying decisions are emotional ones that are justified by logic afterward. Why don't we know this about teaching theology?

Believing is a *heart* issue. Our heart is the very core of who we are. Our head can only agree with what our heart already believes. Faith does not come from the head but from the heart.

Here's what Paul said:

> For **with the heart one believes** unto righteousness, and with the mouth confession is made unto salvation. (Rom. 10:10)

Do we see the correlation here? We believe with our heart and confess what we *already* believe in our heart with our mouth (head). It's not that we shouldn't study or think deeply about God; it's that it's from the heart that one believes.

This is why stories and songs are remembered more than facts, even if the songs and stories are outright lies. When they touch our heart, we tend to believe them more deeply. When Luther started the Protestant Reformation, it was the songs he wrote that ignited the hearts of the people and fueled the reformation fire, not his systematic theology. Music is hard-wired into who you and I are as a person.

Perhaps we should be communicating who God is to the heart first and explain it to the head afterward. God is most deeply understood in our heart-felt encounters with Him. Revelation precedes explanation. This is the way God made us. Everything flows from God through our heart to our head.

THE ART AND SOUL OF GOD

I've always liked impressionism. I think one of the reasons is that this art genre seems to express the heart more than the head. These artists aren't trying to duplicate exactly what they see with technical precision but seek to capture the soul of what they see.

Maureen and I used to visit the Art Institute a lot when we lived in Chicago and still visit when we can. I can spend hours enjoying Degas, Monet, Renoir, Van Gogh, Lautrec, Seurat, Pissarro and the others. These artists seem to have captured the heart and soul of humanity — something wired deep in all of us by the Master Painter Himself.

Vincent Van Gogh once said, *"I want to touch people with my art. I want them to say 'he feels deeply, he feels tenderly.'"* [20] I think this is exactly what our heavenly Father wants to show us in His creation—*how deeply and tenderly He feels toward us.*

God is a *creator*, not a technician. Everything about Him flows like perfect poetry. And *you* are His masterpiece, sculpted from heaven for glory!

> For **we are God's masterpiece.** He has created us anew
> in Christ Jesus, so we can do the good things he planned
> for us long ago. (Eph. 2:10 NLT)

The glory of God is best contemplated with childlike fascination and wild-eyed wonder while lying barefoot in the grass under a starry summer night. For He is the ultimate artist and the universe is His canvas. It speaks volumes about the One who lavishly paints endlessly diverse sunsets and who the poets of Scripture tell us spreads out the galaxies like a tapestry before us.

God is a creator, not a technician.

Consider that we can probably only see a few hundred stars on the clearest and darkest of nights, yet He gave us hundreds of millions of stars and just about as many galaxies. *That* is over-the-top extravagance!

A PERSONAL WALTZ WITH GOD

It's been said that the universe was created to the rhythm of the waltz. All of creation spins and flows to the graceful rhythms of this Divine Dance between the Father, Son, and Spirit that has been going on from eternity. Can you sense the graceful rhythms of His love? Can you hear Him singing over you with joy?[21] Can you feel the Father moving with you, holding you, as you dance this eternal dance of unfathomable love with Him?

I actually had an encounter like this with the Father during worship at a conference I attended. I was standing and singing with everyone else and I happened to be swaying. All of a sudden, I became very aware of what felt like my heavenly Papa swaying with me, His great big arms of love wrapped around me. Not only that, but I could hear Him singing over me in my spirit! I just collapsed in my chair and was a liquid mess for the rest of the meeting, overwhelmed in His love.

These moments with God teach me more about Him and resonate more deeply than anything I have ever studied. But because of these love encounters, when I study the Bible it comes vibrantly alive in full color with His love. I absolutely love reading the Bible *because it's full of Him* and satisfies my heart, yet I always hunger for more!

This is the wonderful paradox of entering into this reciprocating love relationship with God. This is knowing Him, yet always wanting to know Him more.

THE TRUTH STILL MAKES US FREE

Of course, the problem with the heart is that it can sentimentalize and romanticize who God is into oblivion and never touch the truth of who He is. Instead of creating a god according to our intellect, we create a god according to our sentiments.

Furthermore, the problem with artistic expression—especially with music or poetry where words are used, is that the songwriter or poet can get it terribly wrong. Indeed, I have often told my congregation that we should never get our theology from popular Christian songs. They are often full of existential sentimentalities and orphan-hearted thinking that can create a greater conflict between who we truly are in Christ and who we "feel" we are in Him.

But my point is still valid. In fact, this questionable influence makes my point. The message, even if it's wrong, goes much deeper through the heart than through the head.

The truth of God's Word is critical to renewing our mind by faith. It's how we take captive thoughts that try to argue against what God says about us.[22] Even so, truth is more deeply believed and better understood through the heart.

Filling our heads with truth without regularly experiencing deep encounters of the heart with God only makes us critical, divisive, and pharisaical.

HOW'S YOUR THEOLOGY WORKING FOR YOU?

The genius of God regarding our theology is that He lets us walk it out and see if it works. God let me walk out my theology for 20-plus years until it all came crashing down. This is why our understanding of God must be constantly examined. Our old thinking should be challenged and adjusted as we look for better understanding.

As I said in the beginning of this book, we're not dismissing everything that came before us; we're building on its foundation. We let God remove *"those things that are being shaken, as of things that are made, that the things which cannot be shaken may remain."*[23]

So my question for you is this. Does your theology actually work in your everyday life? I'm not asking if it makes sense to your head. I'm asking, does it consistently endear your heart to the Father in Christ and produce the fruit of the Spirit—love, peace, joy, patience, kindness, goodness, faithfulness, gentleness, and self-control? [24]

Does your theology reveal God *in all your relationships*? In your family? Your marriage? Your work place? When all hell breaks loose in your life? If our theology doesn't transform our everyday "stuff," then it needs to change! That's called *re*-formation, and reformation is always about upgrade, which is one of the Holy Spirit's specialties!

As Charles Caleb Colton once said, *"Life isn't like a book. Life isn't logical or sensible or orderly. Life is a mess most of the time. And theology must be lived in the midst of that mess."*[25]

CHAPTER FOUR ENDNOTES

[1] From an essay by C.S. Lewis *"The Seeing Eye"* (originally called, *"Onward, Christian Spacemen")* published in *Show Magazine* (February, 1963)

[2] Dr. C. Baxter Kruger, Perichoresis Inc.

[3] I discuss what I mean by an "orphan mindset" in chapter one.

[4] See Hebrews 1:1-4

[5] Matthew 5:21, 27, 33

[6] From 1951 movie, based on Dickins' *A Christmas Carol*. Quote retrieved at http://www.cedmagic.com/featured/christmas-carol/1951-xmas-fan.html

[7] Jonathan Edwards, "Sinners in the Hands of an Angry God. A Sermon Preached at Enfield, July 8th, 1741." (1741). Smolinski, Reiner, Editor, *Electronic Texts in American Studies*. Paper 54., 15

[8] Luke 7:34

[9] See Mark 15:34

[10] See Isaiah 53:4

[11] See Matthew 12:28-29; Luke 13:16; Acts 10:38; 2 Corinthians 4:4; 1 Peter 5:8; 1 John 5:19

[12] See John 3:16

[13] See 1 John 4:8

[14] For information about the Nicene Creed, go to Theopedia at: http://www.theopedia.com/Nicene_Creed

[15] See Ephesians 3:15

[16] Ep. CI, To Cledonius the Priest Against Apollinarius; NPNF Series 2 Vol. VII, 440

[17] See Romans 6:3-4; Ephesians 2:6; Colossians 3:3

[18] C. Baxter Kruger, "The Trinitarian Vision Summary" (2012). Retrieved at http://baxterkruger.blogspot.com/2012/09/summary-of-trinitarian-vision.html

[19] See Psalm 16:11; 36:8

[20] From "99 Inspirational Artist Quotes" (#52). Retrieved at http://www.artpromotivate.com/2012/09/famous-inspirational-art-

quotes.html.

[21] See Zephaniah 3:17

[22] See 2 Corinthians 10:3-5

[23] See Hebrews 12:27

[24] Galatians 5:22-23

[25] Quote retrieved at: http://www.brainyquote.com/quotes/authors/c/charles_caleb_colton_2.html?vm=l

LOVE SHIFT

"Oh! What would make her waken?" asked the Queen weeping. "Love," replied the fairy."

-From "Sleeping Beauty"

God is passionately, relentlessly, tenaciously, tirelessly, resolutely determined about this one thing—to awaken love in us. This our heart already knows but our mind still resists. And if we don't find our lives in God's love, we *will* seek after the counterfeit.

Nevertheless, Love will not be thwarted. He's ever wooing us, haunting us and surrounding us with His unshakable, unending, and unfathomable love, waiting for us to come awake to it.

Hear His affections reverberating in the deepest part of your soul...COME AWAKE, MY LOVE!

I slept, but my heart was awake, when I heard my lover knocking and calling, 'Open to me, my treasure, my darling, my dove, my perfect one....' (Song 5:2 NLT)

At a DNA level of who we are as a person, we *must* be loved and love, though some may foolishly try to deny it. Even as a devoted follower of Christ, when we're not abiding in His affections for us, something terrible happens to our soul.

Here's the first thing we need to know. All love originates from God because He *is* love.[1] Therefore, the Love Shift we are to make is going from knowing that we're *supposed* to love God to *knowing* we are loved by Him. It's living in an awareness of the Father's affections and simply reciprocating *His* love.

> *I've found that if I let Him hold my heart, I can give it away to you. You cannot hurt what He is holding.*

I think most of us are afraid to love intimately because we could get hurt. Many of us have been deeply hurt by others when we finally did open our heart. Love means risk. Maybe this will help you take courage here. I've found that if I let Him hold my heart, I can give it away to you. You cannot hurt what He is holding. So, don't be afraid. Let it all go. Give it to Him to hold for you. You can truly find rest in His embrace.

So, how do we rest in His embrace? Let's look at something I think will help us with that.

DOES *HIS* PERCEPTION OF YOU OCCUPY YOUR AFFECTIONS?

A group of us were gathered in my living room one night talking about what we had just heard. We were listening to the first track of Graham Cooke's Devotional Soaking series, *Becoming the Beloved.* We have used this CD series in our discipleship and ministry school for a couple of years now. They are transformational, to say the least. But there was a particular line that struck a couple of us this time, *"It is My perception of you that must occupy your affections."* [2]

It is HIS perception, what *God* sees when He looks at you; it's His appraisal that must inform your heart. It's not what you think about yourself, nor how people love you or see you or what they may say about you. Not even how well you love God or how well you serve Him. It's not based on those things at all.

Your heart must be tuned to HIS view of you.

This is the key to a life well lived and loved, because our life always comes down to the issues of our heart.[3]

We know the commandment that covers all commandments is to love God with all our heart, soul, mind, and strength.[4] I asked my church family one time, *"How many of you have honestly obeyed this one commandment? How many have actually loved God with all your heart, soul, mind, and strength?"* Not one person, including myself, raised his or her hand. None of us could say we even fully obeyed this one commandment!

Have you done this consistently? Honestly?

So what are we to do?

First, we must know that we will only ever successfully love God this way because He loves us this way—*with all HIS heart, soul, mind, and strength?*[5] What does God loving *you* with all of HIS heart look like? With all of HIS soul, mind, and strength? Because this reality is HIS perception of you! We will look at this further in a moment.

We're also told it's equally important to love others the same way we love ourselves.[6]

Love *ourselves?*

How does one do that successfully? Selflessly? Obediently? Affectionately? Again, His perception of us is the key.

We determine in our hearts only to see ourselves the way *He* sees us and to love the truth about ourselves. If He loved us and placed such value on us that He gave Jesus for us, who are we to argue? Jesus loved this way. He tells us that He loves us exactly the same way the Father has loved Him:

> As the Father loved Me, I also have loved you; abide in My love. (John 15:9)

And that the Father loves us the same way He loves Jesus:

I in them, and You in Me; that they may be made perfect in
one, and that the world may know that You have sent Me,
and have loved them as You have loved Me. (John 17:23)

Did you get that? God loves *you* the *same* as He loves Himself. And just how much is that? Well, how much does God love God? Can words even begin to describe or quantify it? Let that wonderful thought deeply resonate in your heart.

Furthermore, this unfathomable love speaks of value. How much value do you have to God if He paid Jesus…*for you*? To make this more concrete, say the following to yourself, inserting your name where it normally says "the world":

*For **God** (Father) **so loved** _____ (insert your name) **that***
***He gave His only begotten Son**, that whoever believes in*
Him should not perish but have everlasting life. (John 3:16)

The word "world," that you replaced with your name, is the Greek word *kosmos*, which, in this context, means people. You're a person, so you qualify!

> *It's in this*
> *unfathomable love*
> *and infinite value*
> *that we can find love*
> *for ourselves and our*
> *true worth.*

But God doesn't just love you generically, among seven billion other people. No, He has the ability to love you *specifically and uniquely*. While we could only have one favorite child, God can have unlimited favorites!

When John, the apostle, referred to himself as *"the disciple whom Jesus loved,"* [7] he wasn't being boastful or saying he was more loved than the others; he was referring to his *identity*. And you could say exactly the same thing. You are the one whom Jesus loves! You are God's favorite son or daughter! For God is love and you and I are loved by Love. This is who we are at the deepest heart level.

We need to understand that the Father's love is a very different love than simply having great affection. We get a small glimpse into this difference as a parent. What I mean is that there's a vast difference between someone loving children and the love they feel for their own child. Maureen and I have three sons. I still remember how overwhelmed I was when I held each of them in my arms for the first time. I thought, not only do I love them so much that I would do anything for them, *they belong to me. They are part of me! My blood is flowing in their veins. My DNA is in their DNA!*

Beloved child of God, this is just a small glimpse into how the Father loves you. You are part of Him and you belong to Him! You are His child and His heavenly DNA is intertwined with your spiritual DNA.

When we receive only His perception of us...then, and only then, can we truly and rightly love others.

It's in *this unfathomable love and infinite value* that we can find love for ourselves and our true worth. It's not found in our looks, pedigree, talents, ability to perform, or what other people have said about us. It's in how our heavenly Father sees us.

Do you see now why it's the very height of foolishness and utter ignorance to call yourself a worthless worm? To believe that you are nothing and have no value? This darkened image of ourselves takes time to shed—it must be peeled back like an onion, layer after layer, until we finally find ourselves in the very heart of the Father's affections.

When Jesus was saying that we are to love God with all of our heart, soul, mind, and strength, in the command was the promise of providing all of *His* heart, soul, mind, and strength to do it. It's living *from* our placement inside of Christ, in that perfect reciprocating, unchanging love between the Father and His Son, where we learn to be loved and to love. This is called "abiding in Christ."

When we receive only His perception of us, letting His thoughts occupy our affections, then, and only then, can we truly and rightly love others. As John told us, Jesus' commandments here aren't something tedious or burdensome,[8] not something based on our perception or our valuation...*but His.*

We love with *His* love.

Beloved, *whose* perception is guiding your affections? Tune your heart to His heart. Believe what He says about you. Don't accept anything else. This is true repentance, which is recalibrating your thoughts to His thoughts, beholding Him, embracing His affections and being transformed into who He has already made you.[9]

HOW MUCH DOES GOD THINK ABOUT YOU?

King David understood this about God's valuation of him, with this effusive declaration of His over-the-top affections in Psalm 139:

> *How precious also are Your thoughts to me, O God! How great is the sum of them!* ***If I should count them, they would be more in number than the sand....*** *(Psalm 139:17-18)*

Just for fun, if God's thoughts about you and me are more than the sand, just how much is that? According to David Blatner in his book, *Spectrums*, a group of researchers at the University of Hawaii tried to calculate the number of grains of sand there are on the earth. Here's what they came up with:

> If you assume a grain of sand has an average size and you calculate how many grains are in a teaspoon and then multiply by all the beaches and deserts in the world, the Earth has roughly 7.5×10^{18} grains of sand, or **seven quintillion, five hundred quadrillion grains of sand.**[10]

What David was trying to express in the psalm is that God has *more* than 7,500,000,000,000,000,000 thoughts about you!

We are also told that God's thoughts toward you and me are *good* thoughts, full of hope and peace.

For I know the thoughts that I think toward you, says the Lord, thoughts of peace and not of evil, to give you a future and a hope. (Jer. 29:11)

Let's put this in perspective.

Suppose that God wanted to share one of His good thoughts that He has about you every second of your life, starting from the day of your birth until the day you die. There are about 31,557,600 seconds in a year. If you lived to be 80 years old, and God shared one of His good thoughts about you every second of your life, it would only exhaust 0.0000027% of the total number. In fact, you would still have 2,970,758,230 more years to go, just to get to the "grains of sand" level of God's total number of good thoughts of hope and peace for you!

Of course, the psalmist states that God's thoughts toward us are *more* than the sand, so we're probably grossly underestimating here.

That's something to think about.

Dearest sought-out one, God cannot stop thinking about you. You are in His thoughts continuously, whether you're aware of it or not. He saw you when you were wounded by others and how that caused you to close your heart to intimacy, when you felt betrayed and abandoned, when you cried out in the night, when you felt alone, when God seemed so distant. The truth is, His eyes are steadfastly on you and His heart is forever for you. Always remember that He gave of Himself, in the person of the incarnated Son He dearly loved, so that you could know this Ultimate Love

CAN UNCONDITIONAL LOVE HAVE CONDITIONS?

Accepting that God's love is unconditional is another Love Shift that many sincere believers need to make. You would think this is obvious and needs no further explanation since God *is* love, yet so many still struggle with this. In fact, some have even taught that God's love depends on our response or behavior.

The belief that God's love is conditional is at the root of all performance-based Christianity. This is also probably one of the most demonic lies of all because it puts a question mark on God's emphatic declaration of His love for us.

When we create doctrines that God's love is conditional, we're projecting our own self-focused and fickle human distortion of love on to God. We've made it all about us, but God's love is all about Him.

Here are a few thoughts on God's love, in addition to what we've already talked about.

First, we know that God *is* love.

God = Love. Love is a proper noun here.

Love is God's identity.

John also says in the same epistle that this is how we know God — if we love. We cannot know God and not know love. If we don't love, we prove that we don't know God.

> *The belief that God's love is conditional is at the root of all performance-based Christianity.*

God cannot love you anymore or any less than He loves Himself. His love is always full-on. It's always blazing, white hot. If you want to experience more of God's love, simply draw near and open your heart like you would warm yourself next to a fully stoked open blast furnace.

We also know from Scripture that there is no one or nothing greater than God. We also understand that unconditional love is superior to conditional love. From this biblical premise, we can know for certain that God's love is unconditional for four reasons.

First, if God is love, He can only give love because that's who He is. Second, God cannot have both conditional love and unconditional love. The former negates the possibility of the latter. Third, we know that God does not show any partiality in anything He does, so He doesn't love some and not love others.[11] Finally, it would be impossible for anyone to exhibit unconditional love if God's love is conditional, because that would mean they could do something God could not, love unconditionally. I don't think we want to make that case.

As already stated, *we* make God's love conditional when our view of our relationship with Him is performance-driven. As long as we see ourselves as a dutiful slave instead of a beloved son or daughter, we won't understand God's unconditional love.

If we don't know who we are, we will believe the lie of all lies that haunts the deepest part of our souls, *"I must do something so that God will love me."* We might not say it in those words, but our actions and reactions say it just the same.

But God does not love like we do. This is also why we need to express *His* steadfast and unchanging love, instead of the fickle and thin-skinned version we've called love. He gave us His Spirit so we could love Him and others with His love and without our conditions. The Father declared over Jesus, *"This is My beloved Son in whom I am well pleased"*[12] before Jesus started His ministry. This shows that love is not dependent on performance.

Beloved child of God, your heavenly Father says the same thing over you, apart from anything you could ever do for Him. He is saying over you right now, *"You are My son/daughter, in whom I am well pleased."* Can you receive it? Can you just *be* loved, without any need to perform or win approval?

God's love is unconditional, which means it has no conditions.

CAN YOU HAVE LOVE WITHOUT FREE WILL?

Another area we may need to shift our thinking about love is in our understanding of God's sovereignty. My personal view is that there has been much misunderstanding in *how* God uses His sovereignty, and this has caused a lot of unnecessary confusion and even anger toward

God. It also keeps us from understanding how love works in all relationships.

Sovereignty simply means supreme rule or authority. God definitely has supreme rule over His creation. But if God is sovereign, it also means that He can do *whatever* He wants, right? He's not bound to do, or not do, anything. With this in mind, remember that God is love, and He's primarily about relationship and family. So here's the key. How God *chooses* to exercise His sovereignty is determined by love.

> *How God chooses to exercise His sovereignty is determined by love.*

This is why God, in His sovereignty, *arbitrarily* chose to make us in His image so we could freely choose to partner with Him on the earth and not be mindless automatons who just follow orders. We see this sovereign purpose in His unrescinded mandate for man to have dominion over the earth.[13] Furthermore, as the Psalmist says, He has given *us* the earth.

> *The highest heavens belong to the Lord, but the earth he has given to mankind. (Psalm 115:16 NIV)*

Why would God do this? Because of love! To fully experience love *requires* reciprocation between free persons. So God has sovereignly chosen to give us free will. He did so because He has the right to do so, and His motive to do so is love.

God has also determined to give us autonomy in Him. This was intended to be an *interdependent* relationship, not an independent one. For instance, when Adam was given the assignment by God to name the animals, he could pick the names himself. God wanted the animals to have names, but Adam had the freedom to choose those names.

It was this autonomy that allowed Adam to choose to eat the forbidden fruit of the Tree of the Knowledge of Good and Evil and, thus, break his interdependent relationship with God. Adam and Eve freely chose to doubt God's intentions for them, and so they partnered with Satan, choosing independence instead. Jesus freely chose to trust God and, thus, reversed what Adam had done to our relationship with God.[14]

God has given mankind the earth to manage and take care of because of His love. He honors us by giving us free will—even to hate Him if we so choose, for God still loves us as He loves Himself.

DOES GOD CHANGE TOWARD YOU?

When we talk about God not changing, we need to understand in what way that's meant. The Bible gives us clues to discover this throughout. This non-changing of God, in its proper context, does not mean that God is some statue-like deity who has no interaction with us. Quite the opposite. While He never changes in His nature or character or love for us, He very much gives us room to interact with Him and even change events in this life.

This is reflected in how I am unswerving in my love for my children. My affection for them never changes, and their value to me and my desire for relationship with them never changes. But this same love for them also greatly influences me to change my mind, in certain given situations, and how I interact with them. This is because I want to honor their need to grow as free persons. Obviously, this happens a lot in our ongoing relationships with our children, and it happened a lot in man's interaction with God in Scripture and in our own lives.

This is why God wants us to pray. Prayer is how we interact with God—sharing what's on our heart with Him, and He with us.

A lot of people struggle with God because of all the suffering that is experienced on the earth. While this subject is beyond the scope of this book, I will say here that I think most people have a wrong understanding of God and how He interacts with us. I know I did.

We assume that because He *can* do anything, He *should* do it. But this would violate love, so, instead He gives mankind the free will to run things the way we want. You could say that God governs by *consent*. Of course, we like free will and consent when it benefits us; we get angry when it doesn't.

This is the risk God takes because of love and the price of free will. We can choose to either reciprocate His love or reject His love and even hate Him. But think about it. Doesn't the right to choose, even with all the obstacles, make life worthwhile?

We can't have it both ways. Either we are mindless slaves or we are free people, capable of expressing great love or great evil. When we understand this, we would never want it any other way. Especially when we understand how much God cherishes us and passionately loves us.

THE DIVINE EXCHANGE: OUR TREASURE AND HIS PEARL OF GREAT PRICE

I'm convinced that what is at the very center of God's plan of redemption is in the intimate and profound exchange between the Creator of the Universe and the object of His great affection — us.

We get a glimpse of this exchange in two parables of Jesus — the hidden treasure in the field and the pearl of great price. First, I want to mention that Jim Neeley has some brilliant insights about this in his book, *The Romance of Grace.* I would highly recommend this book. I will contribute my own thoughts here. These two short parables are all about discovery, beauty, absolute passion and ultimate fulfillment. And it's certainly about transformation into the life God meant for us.

The treasure in the field. Before we can understand this parable about hidden treasure, we need to ask ourselves, *what* is our treasure? Let me help you find out what it is with the following illustration.

Imagine that everything in your life is in your house. If this house were to catch fire and you could only save one thing, what would that one thing be?

Whatever that one thing is, would be your treasure.

Now, if I were talking to you face-to-face, you might give me the "Christian" answer you think I would want to hear. That's how we've been trained to respond.

But the bare-naked truth is your treasure is what you hold on to when all hell breaks loose in your life and answers seem nowhere in sight. Your treasure is what you won't give up when something has to go in your busy schedule.

You will do without a lot of things, but you will *never* do without your treasure.

This is what Jesus meant when He said that our treasure is where our heart is.[15] It locates us. And our heart is a funny thing. It doesn't lie about our treasure. We may say otherwise with our mind, even convince everyone else around us. But our heart is like a precision compass, always pointing true north—to what we value most.

This is what Jesus meant when He said that our treasure is where our heart is. It locates us.

I point this out because this is at the very center of why so many blood- bought children of God struggle in their walk with Christ. Why their Christian experience seems like a roller-coaster ride—going up and down, full of spins and turns—yet never really going anywhere. I should know. I had a ticket on that roller coaster for about 23 years!

Because, when your ship seems to be sinking, when your life seems to be falling apart, *you will always hang on to who or what you value most.* And unfortunately for many Christians, at these times, it's their daily relationship with Christ or the fellowship in His family (called the church) that gets thrown overboard. This is because, even though they've given their life to Christ, they've never found their true treasure in Him. Here's what Jesus said about it:

> *Again, the kingdom of heaven is like treasure hidden in a field, which a man found and hid; and for joy over it he goes and sells all that he has and buys that field. (Matt. 13:44)*

I want you to notice the response of the man who finds this kingdom treasure. It's one of *joy* and *total abandon*. Have you ever been head-over-heels in love? This is getting close to what it's like to find this treasure. You're so full of joy that nothing else matters. You don't care what your friends, family, or anyone else thinks, you're totally beside yourself—crazy in love. By the way, this is why the Greek philosophers thought falling in love was a form of insanity!

On the other hand, if you came to Christ because you wanted to escape hell, the Great Tribulation, or maybe you just wanted Jesus to fix the mess you were in, *you still haven't found this treasure.*

You still value other things more…like self-preservation.

And you might've even been told to "surrender all" to Christ, so you attempted to do so, but your heart wasn't really in it. You did it because you're *supposed* to do it. So now you're left feeling guilty and frustrated, caught in a religious performance trap because it's not your treasure. You're living a life full of conflict between what you think you *should* do and what you *really want to do*—which is your treasure.

But as soon as fear of hell is relieved, the rapture didn't happen, or your life gets back into some semblance of order, you may go right back to what you really wanted to do, either in secret or just leaving your commitment to Christ altogether. You give up your conflicted life in Christ for the pleasures you really wanted but can't have.

You can only go against what your heart really wants for so long. What our heart wants is much stronger than what our will forbids.

It might not even be about sin. It might just be about getting busy doing other things rather than passionately pursuing a life in Christ. But it's always about passionately pursuing your treasure.

Understand that this struggle you're experiencing is simply because you still haven't found this treasure in the field that Jesus is talking about.

Furthermore, this heart conflict is by God's design. He created you for passion and desire and fulfillment. Trying to be controlled by head-knowledge and self-determination is a human imitation and not the life meant for you in Christ.

No matter what your treasure is right now, you will only be satisfied with the *true* treasure. While you may pursue counterfeit passions in order to satisfy your God-ordained need for fulfillment, your soul is haunted by something you know is out there but you haven't yet found.

But when you finally do discover this hidden treasure in the field — this light shining out of darkness *"who has shone in our hearts to give the light of the knowledge of the glory of God in the face of Jesus Christ"*[16] — no one has to guilt trip you into giving up everything for it. In fact, they may say the opposite; they may try to dial you down and say you're going too far. But no one or anything will stop you because your heart's on fire and every cell in your body seems to be singing; you must have this treasure at *any* cost.

A life filled with joy and total abandon is all about finding this treasure that God has hidden *for* us.

The pearl of great price. I said at the beginning that the very center of God's plan of redemption is found in the intimate and profound exchange of affections between God and us. Now, let's look at the other side of this mutual exchange. Again, Jesus masterfully describes it in the next parable that follows the one we just looked at:

> *Again, the **kingdom of heaven** is like a **merchant** seeking beautiful pearls, who, **when he** had found one **pearl of great price**, went and **sold all that he had and bought it**. (Matt. 13:45-46)*

Okay, let's start by getting the characters straight in this story. The story clearly defines them, but you're going to need to pretend like you're reading it for the first time.

Who is the "merchant" seeking precious pearls here?

The kingdom of heaven.

Who is the "he" who bought this "pearl of great price?"

The merchant.

Who, then, is this "pearl of great price?"

You are.

Back to the parable, *who is seeking out whom here?* Heaven is seeking *you* out. Do you see it? If not, read it again…slowly…as if for the first time.

I remember when I first heard my brother-in-law, Tim Cummuta, share this view a few years back in a message at our local church. I don't know why I didn't see it before; it's so clear to me now. I was always taught that Jesus was the Pearl of Great Price…that is, until I actually read what He said through the Father's eyes of love.

> *While your treasure is what you won't do without and value most, what God won't do without and what He values most is you.*

That's a Love Shift!

You see, while your treasure is what you won't do without and value most, what God won't do without and what He values most is *you*. The Kingdom is meant to be your treasure because you are HIS pearl of great price. This is at the very center of God's eternal plan of redemption—this mutual exchange of great affections between us and God. Let me say it another way.

Imagine there was a most wealthy and powerful king who wanted you above everything else. But even though he could have anything his heart desired, because of love, he would never force his affections on you by his power. So he waits for your response to His overture, with indefatigable hope, so that he can give himself completely to you and pour His love out on you.

Beloved, there is such a King, and He is your heavenly Father! He gave everything. He bankrupted heaven to free you from a wicked prince who held you in his loveless dudgeon where you were left in the dark and continuously haunted by two questions...

"Am I alone?" and *"Do I matter?"*

Do you hear what I'm saying? You are loved! You will *never* be alone and you *do* matter most of all! You, my precious friend, are a most beautiful and lustrous pearl that God has been seeking out from before the foundation of the world. And I contend that part of the reason we struggle with the treasure in the field—the Kingdom of God—is because we don't understand that we are His pearl of great price.

> *When you finally see that you are God's precious pearl, you will begin to see the hidden treasure of the Kingdom*

Because of His deep other-centered love, God removes everything that could stand between your discovery of His treasure and finding your value in Him. This is at the heart of why God does what He does.

After all, your heavenly Father gave everything for you by giving what was most valuable and precious to Him—His only begotten Son, Jesus. And what did Jesus do? *"For the joy set before Him,"*[17] He took upon Himself all of our pain, our incredible sadness, our feelings of abandonment, betrayal, rejection, bitter disappointment, anger, hatred, our bondages and addictions, *our* enmity against God—every poisonous infection in our soul and everything that blinded us to what is real.

Why did Jesus do this? Because of love! So we could finally see Him rightly, want Him fully, and enjoy the life He lives abundantly, with Him and His Father forever. He took our death to the grave so we could find our life in Him. And that life is waiting for you to see this.

When you finally see that you are God's precious pearl, you will begin to see the hidden treasure of the Kingdom. For this is what you've been invited into, and it's your Father's good pleasure to give it all to you, if you will receive it.[18]

One more thing. Why did Jesus use a pearl in this story? Why not use diamonds or some other more precious stone? I believe it was because, unlike other precious stones that we may value more in this world, pearls come from living things. And, of all living things in all creation, you are most precious to Him.

Precious one, YOU are SO loved!

CHAPTER FIVE ENDNOTES

[1] See 1 John 4:8

[2] Graham Cooke, "Devotional Soaking Series." *Becoming the Beloved*, Part 1. Brilliant Book House Publishing.

[3] See Proverbs 4:23

[4] See Mark 12:30

[5] See 1 John 4:19

[6] Mark 12:31

[7] See John 19:26; 20:2; 21:7, 20

[8] See 1 John 5:13

[9] See Romans 12:2; 2 Corinthians 3:18

[10] Quote retrieved from http://www.npr.org/sections/krulwich/2012/09/17/161096233/which-is-greater-the-number-of-sand-grains-on-earth-or-stars-in-the-sky

[11] See Acts 10:34

[12] See Luke 3:22

[13] See Genesis1:26-28

[14] See Romans 5:18-19

[15] Matthew 6:21

[16] 2 Corinthian 4:6

[17] See Hebrews 12:2

[18] See Luke 12:32

CHAPTER SIX

IDENTITY SHIFT

But what did he see in the clear stream below? His own image; no longer a dark, gray bird, ugly and disagreeable to look at, but a graceful and beautiful swan.

- From "The Ugly Duckling" [1]

You've probably read or least have heard of the wonderful fairytale called "The Ugly Duckling" by Hans Christian Andersen. I think God can speak to us profoundly through this tale about our own identity. Here's a good summary of the story:

> The story tells of a homely little bird born in a barnyard who suffers abuse from the others around him until, much to his delight (and to the surprise of others), he matures into a beautiful swan, the most beautiful bird of all. [2]

I will focus in on the ending of the story to lay a foundation for the Identity Shift we need to make. In this scene, in final desperation, the ugly duckling approaches some swans in the water nearby. As he approaches with fear and dread, he glances down at his reflection for the first time and is instantly confused and delighted by what he sees.

What happens next is transformational. Here's an excerpt from the story; the children feeding the swans see him approach:

"See," cried the youngest, "there is a new one;" and the rest were delighted, and ran to their father and mother, dancing and clapping their hands, and shouting joyously, "There is another swan come; a new one has arrived.

Then they threw more bread and cake into the water, and said, "The new one is the most beautiful of all; he is so young and pretty." And the old swans bowed their heads before him.

Then he felt quite ashamed, and hid his head under his wing; for he did not know what to do, he was so happy, and yet not at all proud. He had been persecuted and despised for his ugliness, and now he heard them say he was the most beautiful of all the birds. Even the elder-tree bent down its bows into the water before him, and the sun shone warm and bright. Then he rustled his feathers, curved his slender neck, and cried joyfully, from the depths of his heart, "I never dreamed of such happiness as this, while I was an ugly duckling."[3]

So what does this mean to us?

This story is so much like our story.

I respectfully submit that what most of us have experienced thus far is an "ugly duckling" version of Christianity. It's certainly has not been one that's transformational. We've been living like we were ugly ducklings all our lives. And like this ugly duckling, we don't know who we are though we think we do.

I would guess you've tried to fit in the "ugly duck" world, but it left you feeling alone, abused, and starving for true love. You may have even joined an "ugly duck" church but it, too, left you out in the cold, starving on a steady diet of powerless duck religion.

It fed you on a steady diet of "being a better duck" principles, yet you're feeling like a failure. While you might understand change is necessary, no amount of guilt and manipulation is going to change you.

Why? Because you can't become a most beautiful swan by being told you're a dirty ugly duckling.

But in your final desperation, you happen upon this hidden place. It is there that you see the beautiful scene before you and finally gaze upon your true self. At first you hide in shame, yet a strange hope begins to fill your heart; you begin to feel a euphoric sense of freedom and purpose for the first time in your life. It just sounds too good to be true, yet there it is before you. Every cell within you is resonating with absolute joy and pure love!

And who are the children and the swans in our story?

The children are the heavenly hosts and the swans are your brethren. This is the family of God. This is where you belong!

Beautiful one, you have come to Mount Zion and to the city of the living God, the heavenly Jerusalem, to an innumerable company of angels, to the general assembly and church of the firstborn who are registered in heaven, to God the Judge of all, to the spirits of just men made perfect. [4] You are home at last! You have found yourself, not only in your Father's embrace, but in His family that exists in both heaven and on the earth.

And like this ugly duckling, we don't know who we are though we think we do.

You've discovered that you belong to the Royal House of God! You have all along. You just never knew about this dream come true. This is a place of endless joy and love — where there is no lack, no sorrow, tears or disappointment. And somehow you know you will never be alone again.

You will never again "not belong" or see yourself as an "I am not." You've been placed inside the Great I AM! You finally know in the deepest part of your heart that you do matter.

This is where you see your true reflection, for this reflection is *God's* estimation of you. It is here in this hidden Kingdom where the Royal

Family affirms your beauty and ultimate worth, for you are the most valued and desired of all His creation.

All of this is found in the Divine exchange, when we finally see His hidden Kingdom "treasure" through our "pearl" eyes! Our response is much like the transformed ugly duckling: "Then he rustled his feathers, curved his slender neck, and cried joyfully, from the depths of his heart, *"I never dreamed of such happiness as this, while I was an ugly duckling."*[5]

ARE YOU SEEING *YOUR* TRUE REFLECTION?

Our Identity Shift is about finally seeing our true reflection in Christ. What do you see when you look at your own reflection? What we *should* be seeing is a reflection of Jesus.

Do you understand what this means? It means that the only person we can legitimately identify with in the gospel stories where Jesus is ministering is Jesus—not the sick and demon-possessed who came to receive from Him, not even His disciples (before His resurrection and their reception of the Holy Spirit).

> *The truth is, there's nothing you can add to who you already are in Him.*

For as the Father sent Jesus, He is sending you to be just as He was.[6]

Does this all sound like a fairytale to you? It's the most real thing there is, but you need to choose what you will believe: what God says about you or what you think about yourself.

We must overcome the damage that powerless religion has done to our understanding of our true identity in Christ. The truth is, there's nothing you can add to who you *already* are in Him. Paul said we are "complete in Christ."

I will use the Amplified Bible to bring this statement out more clearly. I also want you to notice the relationship between Jesus and you in this passage:

*For **in Him the whole fullness of Deity** (the Godhead)*
***continues to dwell in bodily form** [giving complete ex-*
pression of the divine nature].

***And you are in Him**, made full and having come to full-*
*ness of life [**in Christ you too are filled with the God-***
***head—Father, Son and Holy Spirit**—and reach full*
spiritual stature]. And He is the Head of all rule and au-
thority [of every angelic principality and power]. (Col. 2:9-
10 AMP)

Do you see the connection between you and Christ? What is in Him
is in you! Do you see that you *already* have everything you will ever
have in Christ? Of course, we don't see it all at first because it requires
spiritual illumination. And that's the Holy Spirit's job. He lives in you
to establish your new nature in Christ.

When we look to Christ, the religious veil that has blinded us to our
true self is taken away, and we begin to see who we really are! This is
walking into true freedom. We looked at this transformation process in
chapter three (Disciple Shift) when we looked at 2 Corinthians 3:18.
Again, *who do you see when you look into a mirror?* You see YOU! Likewise, in this "Holy Spirit" mirror, you begin to see your true reflection
in Christ.

You actually begin to believe what *God* believes about you.

Like with the ugly duckling, as the Father's adopted sons, co-heirs
with Christ, we are starting to see our true reflection in what God says
about us. As we see ourselves in Christ, we are being changed into the
same image from glory to glory! Beloved, you are not an ugly duck;
you're a beautiful swan!

THE WORST IDENTITY THEFT OF ALL

There is an identity theft that's vastly more insidious and destruc-
tive than losing what it says about you in your wallet. What I'm talking
about is the empty religion of man's imagination that contradicts what

God says about us and, therefore, robs us of our true identity in Christ. This is actually tragic—a fraudulent crime perpetrated against God's beloved children.

One thing about our current version of popular Christianity that's just astonishing to me is this lack of understanding of our identity. Here's what I mean.

While we all may readily identify with the death, burial, and resurrection of Christ for our salvation, and rightfully see Him exalted at the right hand of the Father in Heaven, my experience has been that very few Christians seem to be able to identify themselves as dead, buried, and resurrected with Him.[7] Very few actually see themselves seated in Him in heavenly places, far above all principalities and powers.[8]

> *Anything that separates us from Christ is not the gospel but the powerless religion of man's imagination.*

We see Christ, but do we see ourselves *in Him?*

Now, I realize you may nod your head in agreement about our placement in Christ on theological or, perhaps, theoretical grounds. You may even call it our "legal" position. But if this is only a legal standing, then we have no actual life *in* Christ! We are still left outside, still separated from Him, trying to imitate His life. Anything that separates us from Christ is not the gospel but the powerless religion of man's imagination.

Beloved of God, this is the *only* Christian life available to us, even though many seem to think there are other options.

Either we are placed where God says we are or we're not. Let's not let intellectual rhetoric rob us of our glorious inheritance, because what we believe *can* actually launch us into, or keep us from, experiencing the freedom Christ paid for. Paul called the "normal" Christian a *crucified* Christian—a new creation who now lives Jesus' resurrected life.[9] Why do we keep wanting to believe something else?

This is my point. Are you and I followers of Christ? Did we receive Him by grace through faith? Then, if our life is actually Christ's life, which it is, why would we act like powerless victims in this world, living a defeated and hopeless life? Why live like a religious orphan rather than the royal son or daughter of our heavenly Father?

Why are we, Jesus' co-heirs, acting as if we're *ever* separated from Him in any way? After all, we are the hope of the world, because Hope lives in us. To think otherwise is to have our identity stolen from us in the worst possible way.

Furthermore, we've managed to turn these precious promises into something else...meaningless religious gobbledygook. The living Word becomes nothing more than a history book with some inspirational phrases that we can put on plaques to cheer us up and get us through the latest in our unending series of trials.

THE WRONG KIND OF HUMILITY

What do we think it is to be humble? Here's how a spiritual orphan might express it..."*I'm nothing, just a worm in His sight... just a dirty old sinner saved by grace.*"

Does this self-loathing posture sound like true humility to you? Are you embracing a "worthless worm" theology? You might answer, "But isn't our righteousness as filthy rags?" Is it? Paul seemed to think we now have Christ's righteousness.[10] I understand that the intent is to honor Jesus and accentuate the grace of God. That's commendable but dangerously misguided. It actually keeps us locked up in a tomb of doubt and confusion about ourselves, guarded by our own insecurities. It blinds us from seeing who we are on *this* side of the cross of Christ.

True humility, on the other hand, is agreeing with what God says about you—nothing more and nothing less. Anything other than this is not humility. It's just one side of the same two-sided coin of religious pride.

It's not humility to make yourself out to be garbage when God paid the highest possible price for you, nor is it biblical to identify with your old nature. It's actually unbelief, even the very height of arrogance, because we dare to contradict God's estimation of us. And it's demeaning to the glorious nature procured for you by the finished work of Christ.

Degrading yourself devalues what God has accomplished in Christ, for the Father values you the same as He values Jesus, since Jesus is the price He paid for you. And He seems to think that you're His masterpiece, His tapestry—you are *His* workmanship in Christ.

To say otherwise about yourself would be like telling Michelangelo, Rembrandt, or Da Vinci that their works of art are just filthy rags. Actually, it's infinitely worse because you have infinite worth to God.

As Curry Blake[11] has often said… *"Both heaven and hell know who you are; they just want to know if you know who you are."*

You really do need to make a choice if you're going to find out who you truly are in Christ. It's a choice that takes great courage in the face of all the absurd things taught about what it means to be a Christian. But it's also a choice that brings the promise of freedom. Beloved of God, get your identity back. Be a "normal" Christian, which means living Christ's life.[12]

ARE YOU A VOLUNTEER IN SATAN'S PRISON CAMP?

A few years ago, one of the ladies in my congregation shared a dream she had. It was vivid and very instructive. She dreamed she was in what looked like a concentration prison camp with a lot of other captives.

The guards were demons. It was an awful dark and cruel place, and there was this heavy atmosphere of fear, depression, anxiety, hatred, and extreme loneliness even though there were a lot of people there.

As she was walking around the camp, she noticed a lit bulletin board on a wall with various announcements pinned on it. One particular announcement that caught her attention was thanking all the volunteers who were there in the camp. Suddenly, the thought struck her.

"I'm a *volunteer* in Satan's prison camp."

Then she woke up.

We should wake up, too.

The point of the dream was that she should no longer empower Satan's lies about how she sees herself and the world around her. Nor should we.

Our transformation is dependent on how we see ourselves. These lies we believe about ourselves only have the power we give them. We empower Satan's lies by our agreement. The truth is, he cannot rule without our consent.

We give him power when we make him bigger and more powerful in our lives than God and who He says we are in Him. We empower Satan when we fear the supernatural miracle power of God that should be working in and through us, denying it because it could be from the devil. We empower him by seeing ourselves weaker and smaller than he, even though we are actually seated in heav-

> *Our transformation is dependent on how we see ourselves.*

enly places in Christ, which is *far above* all principalities and power, by the way.

Dear chosen one in Christ, you are a royal heir of His eternal Kingdom; don't be a volunteer in Satan's prison camp. He has NO power that you don't give him. Break your agreement with his lies today.

At first, it may take pure faith. The lies will feel real for a while because they have made deep impressions in who you think you are, but they *are* lies, nonetheless. Just determine, from this point forward, to believe God no matter how you feel about it or what it looks like in the natural.

Reality follows faith. Faith in what God says brings us into freedom. Don't let Satan's lies define who you are, whether they come directly from him or from people you know and even love. Don't empower anything that Christ has disempowered on the cross.

LIVING ON THE WRONG SIDE OF THE CROSS

I have found that many Christians, even respected Bible teachers, seem to read the Bible indiscriminately, as though nothing changed because of Jesus. This is especially evident when we read the Old Testament as if the Old Covenant is still binding on us. When we do this, confusion and error are sure to follow, which leads to needless bondage and ignorance about who we are in Christ.

We live on the wrong side of the cross when we're believing things that are no longer true under the New Covenant. Even though these things may have been true before the cross, they're not true now.

We must learn to read Scripture and understand who we are in Christ on THIS side of the cross. Here are just a few of the salient points:

- You are not a sinner saved by grace; you *were* a sinner, now you're a saint saved by grace—a NEW CREATION. There has never been a species in creation like you before Christ (Rom. 1:7; 2 Cor. 5:17; Rom. 8:29; Col. 1:15).
- You do not have a sinful nature; it was crucified with Christ. You are now a partaker in the divine nature, dead to sin (Rom. 6:6; Gal. 2:20; Col. 3:3; 2 Pet. 1:4).
- You are God's adopted son/daughter, not an orphan (Jn. 14:18; Rom. 8:15).
- You are free and not a slave (Mt. 17:26; Gal. 4:6-7).
- You cannot *attain* to holiness; you *obtain* Christ's holiness by faith (Eph. 1:4; Col. 3:12; Heb. 3:1; 1 Pet. 2:5)
- You cannot become righteous, you can only accept Christ's righteousness as a free gift (Rom. 5:17; 2 Cor. 5:21).

- You are God-inhabited flesh; you are His resting place and holy Temple (Acts 7:48-50; 1 Cor. 3:16; 6:19; Eph. 2:6; Col. 1:7; Phil. 3:20).
- What's true about Jesus is true about you in Him. *"As Jesus IS, so are YOU on this earth right now"* (1 Jn. 4:17).
- You are not to consider yourself, or other believers, in any other way but according to Christ (2 Cor. 5:16).

Your life is Christ's life. You're not part of the "Adam's" family anymore! Comparing yourself to Adam, Job, Noah, Moses, Elijah, David, Solomon, John the Baptist, or anyone else under the Old Covenant is living on the wrong side of the cross. The only model you're to follow is that of Christ and Him crucified.

IDENTITY SHIFT: FROM OUR LIFE TO HIS!

The Christian life is not about imitation; it's about *incarnation.* For us to be transformed, we must come into agreement with this fact long before it ever becomes our experience.

Let's look at how this transforms our identity in Christ. Paul seemed to think you *died* with Christ and you are now living in His life:

> *"Or **do you not know** that as many of us as were baptized into Christ Jesus were baptized into His death? Therefore **we were buried with Him** through baptism into death, that **just as Christ was raised from the dead** by the glory of the Father, even so **we also should walk in newness of life**...*
>
> *...**knowing this**, that **our old man was crucified with Him**, that the body of sin might be done away with, that we should no longer be slaves of sin. For he **who has died has been freed** from sin." (Rom. 6:3, 4, 6, 7)*

Our problem comes when we *don't* "know" this.

Are you still considering yourself alive to your sinful nature instead of alive in Christ? Notice that all of these things that God says about you in Christ are *past tense*. There is nothing about this that will ever happen in the future. Your old nature *was* nailed to the cross 2,000 years ago.

There's nothing you can do to change this historical fact but *agree with it* and believe it.

Understand that until we *know* these things we cannot begin to make the Identity Shift needed to free us from our sin-obsessed version of orphan Christianity. This transformation takes place by first agreeing with God's assessment of us, called "reckoning" or "considering" in Romans 6:11. Reckoning is an accounting term. We are "balancing the books" by agreeing with God, believing the same thing He believes about us. Then, we "present" ourselves,[13] by faith, as dead to our old selves and alive in Christ.

> The Christian life is not about imitation; it's about incarnation.

It's all a matter of *who* we will agree with—God or our current experience. Transformation follows identity. For an excellent treatise on this concept, I would highly recommend that you read Watchman Nee's classic work, *The Normal Christian Life*.

ARE WE CRUCIFIED WITH CHRIST OR NOT?

Paul said the following to the Corinthians: *"For I determined not to know anything among you except Jesus Christ and Him crucified."*[14] What did he mean by saying *among you*? I believe He meant that they, and we, should see *ourselves* already dead to sin and crucified with Christ.

This is why trying to "kill our flesh" is like trying to kill a corpse. There is no satisfaction in that because you're *already* dead! Trying to crucify what God has already crucified is an exercise in futility and unbelief. We're like grave robbers, constantly digging up our old stinky dead body of sin, trying to get it to "behave like a Christian." Get out of the cemetery and live in the light of Christ's life! To quote the Coroner of Oz, you're *"not only really dead, you're really most sincerely dead!"*[15]

Our problem is not that our flesh is not dead yet; it's that we don't believe it, so we live like it's still alive.

Paul said that our old sin nature was nailed to the cross, so to say we have two natures not only contradicts this, but it says we're schizophrenic, which is a mental disease! *That is not a normal Christian.* This is not "night of the living dead" either; we're fully alive in Christ! The only thing wrong with us is that we don't fully know it yet. This is why we need our minds renewed according to the finished work of the cross.

What we're actually fighting against is something that's not "us" anymore. Paul saw sin as if it were a foreign body (this "body of sin" Rom. 6:6). For instance, in Romans 6:12, Paul says this:

> *Therefore do not **let** sin reign in your mortal body, that you should obey **it** in **its** lusts.*

Notice two things here. First, sin is an "it." It's not *your* lusts, but *its* lusts. It's foreign to you and your new nature. The second thing to notice is we're not to *"let* sin reign," which means we have complete control over whether or not it will affect us.

Our real problem is an identification problem, not a sin problem.

Picture sin, or even Satan and the powers of darkness, like a dog barking outside your door. He wants you to let him in, but every time you do, he makes a big mess of things. What is the solution? Don't let him in! He can't come inside unless you *let* him in. But also see that the dog is not you. He's a dog, a totally different species and not like you at all.

This is how the New Testament views sin and its influence on us. Our real problem is an *identification* problem, not a sin problem. We're still identifying ourselves on the wrong side of the cross. Rather than praying for God to do something He has already done, we should be praying that the Holy Spirit will help us see what we *already have* in Christ.

Let's leave all our religious baggage behind and start believing what God believes about us and live on the right side of the cross. It's actually pretty amazing.

UGLY DUCKLING CHRISTIANITY SHIFT

One last thought on this Identity Shift. Could it also be that when we finally see our true reflection in Christ, we will also see this world differently? A world that the Father loves so much that He gave Jesus for it? Rather than persecuting us and hating us because of our ugly version of Christianity that didn't look at all like Jesus, they will begin to see the beauty of Jesus shining through us? Just a thought.

> "He had been persecuted and despised for his ugliness, and now he heard them say he was the most beautiful of all the birds. Even the elder-tree bent down its bows into the water before him, and the sun shone warm and bright."

CHAPTER SIX ENDNOTES

[1] Hans Christian Andersen, "The Ugly Duckling." Quote retrieved at http://www.eastoftheweb.com/short-stories/UBooks/UglDuc.shtml

[2] Quote retrieved from Wikipedia at http://en.wikipedia.org/wiki/The_Ugly_Duckling

[3] See note #1

[4] Hebrews 12:22-23

[5] See note #1

[6] See John 14:12; 20:21

[7] See Romans 6:3-6

[8] See Ephesians 1:18-2:6

[9] See 2 Corinthians 5:17; Romans 6:4

[10] See 2 Corinthians 5:21

[11] Curry Blake, John G. Lake Ministries.

[12] See Galatians 2:20

[13] Romans 6:13, 16

[14] 1 Corinthians 2:2

[15] Quote retrieved at http://www.imdb.com/title/tt0032138/quotes?item=qt0409904

GRACE SHIFT

"The Reformation was a time when men went blind, stag-gering drunk because they had discovered, in the dusty basement of late medievalism, a whole cellar full of fifteen-hundred-year-old, two-hundred proof Grace—bottle after bottle of pure distillate of Scripture..."

- Robert Farrar Capon

Sadly, there's nothing intoxicating about a gospel that mixes grace with the law. Paul called it "another gospel," a bewitching brew that doesn't free anyone. [1]

The problem is, the good news, which means "news that brings great joy," just sounds too good to be true, so we dilute it with things we "have to do" to stay in grace because we don't want to give people license to sin. We feel compelled to control behavior through fear (going to hell, going too far to be forgiven, missing the rapture, bad things happening because of disobedience, and so forth.)

The only problem with this is that God compels by His love and empowers self-control by His Spirit of grace.[2]

Like most other believers I knew, for 23 years of my Christian life my perspective on being a Christian amounted to pursuing the fruit of

Spirit-filled living instead of pursuing the Source of Life living in me that produces the fruit. The first thing I did after I gave my heart to Jesus was get a Bible and begin an absurd journey of attempting to obey what it said. I was only doing what everyone else I knew was doing. The sad thing was, I probably felt more freedom in my former rebellion.

Grace, in my mind, was only what saved me. It was God's unmerited favor, which I took to mean getting my "go to heaven" card punched, and as long as I kept it punched by behaving myself and doing good things, I would be okay with God. In other words, now that I was saved, I had to walk it out by my own determination (which I called "spiritual disciplines").

I didn't see that this was what I was doing at the time. After all, my heart *wanted* to obey Jesus. I felt the love of God flooding my soul. I loved everybody! I was free!

As I shared in chapter three (Disciple Shift), my self-determined version of Christianity started to take its toll, which led me on an endless roller coaster ride of frustration, feeling good about myself, followed by more frustration—victories followed by defeat, usually ending up in burn out.

I loved Jesus, but I knew I was not really free. This contradiction just added another layer of frustration because I knew enough to know that freedom is exactly why He came. Even though I knew something was terribly wrong, I didn't understand why at the time. I berated myself for my failures and got very tired of *trying to act like a Christian.*

Pleasing God seemed always out of reach somehow. It was *out there somewhere…if I would just get my act together.*

Then, praise God, I got off the performance treadmill and learned how to just *be* in Him instead of do *for* Him.

I found *Him*…Grace Himself.

How did I make this Grace Shift? For me, it started after my "glorious crash" with deep encounters with the Father's love as I shared in the first chapter. And as I shared in chapter five (Love Shift), I found out that God's unconditional love has no conditions.

I found out that the One who holds everything together, and by whom all things consist...loves *me!* And He still loves me even when I'm at my worst. His constant overflow of love has progressively changed the way I think, because it really does all come down to the way we think—how we think about God and about ourselves.

Identity is critical to understanding grace.

When I saw myself in Him, I went from being a performing slave, groping in the dark for approval, to a fully-affirmed and beloved son, living in the light and love of my Father's embrace.

This is the heart of the Grace Shift I want to talk about here.

ORPHANS DON'T UNDERSTAND PURE GRACE

Spiritual orphans[3] will either abuse or dismiss pure grace. I'm not suggesting that disagreeing with my view of grace automatically makes you a spiritual orphan, but I am saying that spiritual orphans never truly feel loved and affirmed by their heavenly Father, so they will never understand pure, undiluted grace.

> *Spiritual orphans will either abuse or dismiss pure grace.*

I really like the way Jesus' parable about the father and his two sons in Luke 15:11-32 has been taught in recent years. For so long it's been mislabeled the "Parable of the Prodigal Son." It's really about our heavenly Father and the two-sided orphan-hearted reaction to His unconditional love.

As Leif Hetland and others have taught us, the younger prodigal son was the "rebellious" orphan and the elder brother was the "religious" orphan. This description of the two sons can help us understand why spiritual orphans don't embrace pure grace.

The rebellious orphans will abuse this undiluted grace by using it as a pretext for their self-indulgent version of freedom, throwing off the shackles of religious confinement they've perceived as a threat to doing whatever they please. The religious orphan will dismiss this pure grace and warn everyone else to stay away from it, insisting on the shackles of their legalistic mixture of grace and law.

Both the rebellious and religious orphans resist intimacy.

Rebellious orphans have decided to live like a spiritual prodigal, freeing themselves from their negative experiences with church life for a life of no personal accountability or any other perceived restriction on their self-indulgent heart.

On the other hand, "elder brother" religious orphans will dismiss pure grace and keep everyone else from experiencing it through their fear-based theology. They do this by labeling the pure grace teaching as being "sloppy agape" and "greasy grace" or the more recent moniker, "hyper-grace." They define their spirituality by their outward restraint, by what they *don't* do anymore, and by staying inside subjective boundaries they have devised. In reality, they don't trust the Holy Spirit to manage their own behavior, nor do they trust Him to do so in anyone else.

This is at the heart of the challenge we have today in the current wave of fresh grace. Both the rebellious and religious orphans have not been "compelled" to live in God's other-centered love. Their life is marked by embracing salvation from hell but hiding and running away from His love that would bring true freedom to their impoverished souls.

Rebellious orphans separate themselves from God because they are fixated on indulging themselves on what grace allows. Religious orphans separate themselves from God by their constant study of Him, preferring to serve Him as a slave rather than know Him as a son.

Rebellious orphans define freedom as being free from anything that would smack of responsibility or interfere with their self-centered view of life. They look at God as someone who is holding out on them, keeping them locked up in the restraint of religion. The religious orphan defines freedom as being free from sin when they die and go to heaven. The problem with this, of course, is there's no expectation of real freedom in this life.

Both the rebellious and religious orphans resist intimacy: the former does so because it gets in the way of their self-indulgence, and the latter does so because it gets in the way of their self-redemption. They keep Love at a distance because it requires honest heartfelt vulnerability. They want heaven more than they want Who's there. It's all about self-preservation, not love.

One thing is for sure. Neither the rebellious nor the religious orphans understand, nor do they even know, how to embrace real God-distilled grace.

GRACE-HATERS IN THE HANDS OF A RELATIONAL GOD

I agree with Jim McNeely[4] when he says we're all really grace haters at the core of who we are. Just like the elder brother who resented his prodigal brother's gracious homecoming, or like Jonah whining because God didn't punish the wicked Ninevites, or the first worker in the vineyard in Jesus' parable in Matthew 20 who said it wasn't fair that the last worker got paid the same as him.

It's all the same story. We hate grace.

Indeed, the phrase, *"It isn't fair"* is the mantra of a grace hater. We fail to see that the whole point is about relationship rather than "getting paid" or deserving something. This is at the heart of what I believe is one of the biggest reasons why we struggle with the message of God's pure grace.

Ironically, we hate grace whenever someone receives it who we deem is not worthy of it. We hate grace because, even though we're God's fully affirmed sons and daughters, we're still looking for His approval.

We hate grace because everyone gets the *same* grace.

We also hate grace because it goes *both ways*. We love receiving grace when *we* fail, but the thought never occurs to us that we are to extend exactly the same grace to others when they fail to live up to our expectations.

We fail to see that the whole point is about relationship rather than "getting paid" or deserving something.

We won't like these stories as long as we fail to see that the point is not about getting an inheritance or fairness at all; it's about getting the Father. It's about relationship with the Father.

We may try to temper our incensed reaction to this "unfairness" by telling ourselves that we will get more rewards in heaven than those "lazy" and "rebellious" Christians. But keep in mind, the prodigal son did get *all* of his inheritance back, even after squandering it. No probation, no punishment, just full restoration. This won't sit well with you if you think it's all about rewards and retribution.

Even getting greater reward in heaven is still missing the proverbial forest for the trees. As God told Abraham, *"Do not be afraid, Abram. I am your shield, **your exceedingly great reward."** (Gen. 15:1)*

Sadly, payment, rewards, promises and spiritual gifts are more important to the orphan-minded grace hater than being in this moment-by-moment divine union in Christ that we have available to us right now. I don't want to minimize the benefits of our inheritance in Christ and the promises of God. I love the fact that we can do what Jesus did and even greater things. I fully believe that signs and wonders should follow the believer. We should receive all that's ours in Christ by faith.

But all these things, as good as they are, don't begin to compare with the overflowing reality of our "exceedingly great"[5] life in the Father's embrace.

Neither son in the prodigal story wanted a relationship with their father. They wanted his "stuff." The only difference was, the prodigal son wanted what was coming to him right away, and the elder brother was willing to wait until his father died to get his stuff.

This is what Christianity looks like without an abiding relationship—two sides of the same orphan-hearted coin. Inheritance without intimacy.

What we fail to see is that the real benefit of being the prodigal's elder brother, Jonah, or the first worker in the vineyard, was that they were in the relationship longer. This is what it's all about! As the father had to tell the elder brother, *"Son, you are always with me, and all that I have is yours."*[6] And all that our heavenly Father has is a lot!

ARE YOU RUNNING TOWARD GRACE OR LAW?

Now, I would like to talk about untangling God's grace from this deadly mixture of law and grace that we have called grace. To help us see this, I will use an American football analogy. I would like you to picture a football field. At one end zone there is the word "Grace." At the other end zone is the word, "Law." These are the goal lines, if you will. Next, picture an arrow pointing in both directions at the 50-yard line. This arrow represents which direction you may be "taking the ball" at any given moment.

What this football analogy shows us is how grace and Law relate to one another. For instance, as soon as you start heading toward the "Law" end zone, you are moving away from the "Grace" end zone. Conversely, if you run toward the Grace end zone, you are running away from the Law end zone.

Here's how Paul would say it:

For if you are trying to make yourselves right with God by keeping the law, you have been cut off from Christ! You have fallen away from God's grace. (Gal. 5:4 NLT)

What are the lessons we can learn from this football analogy?

- Law and grace are at opposite ends of the field. To head toward one end zone is to move away from the other. This is not to say that the Law is bad. Paul said it was perfect. It was just never meant to make us righteous. It can only expose our unrighteousness.

- If you try to mix the Law with grace in any fashion, you will stay in the middle of the field. You will never score a touchdown, so to speak, which is the goal (your freedom in Christ).

- The only way to score a Grace touchdown is to run all the way down to the opposite end of the field from the Law (and I don't mean become sinful).

While we know that the Law will never bring us freedom, we think that some Law mixed with grace will. For instance, we try to keep the moral Law—the Ten Commandments. This, again, keeps us in the middle of the field going nowhere.

> *While we know that the Law will never bring us freedom, we think that some Law mixed with grace will.*

I have personally worked with people who initially felt some level of freedom by hearing the message of pure grace, but they never let God deal with their orphan heart, so it didn't work for them. They either gave up altogether or took this failure to mean that they needed the structure of the Law to manage them, only to be put into a new prison—a legalistic one.

Understand that the Law was given under the Old Covenant for two reasons. First, as a way of forbearance for Israel's wrongdoing. As Paul tells us in Romans, while bulls and goats could never take away our sins, God overlooked them for a time until

Christ could come. His atoning work on the cross took care of all sin, once and for all.

Second, the Law was an outward restrainer for God's people who were still eating from the Tree of the Knowledge of Good and Evil, which is the way of the flesh. This is because they didn't have the indwelling Holy Spirit to guide them yet. The Law was never meant to make them righteous. It was meant to be their guardian until Christ could become us so we could live in Him.

Grace is how we eat from the Tree of Life (Jesus), which is the way of the Spirit, who then manages us from the inside out. We're no longer managed by the letter of the Law but are being transformed by the Spirit.

> But now we have been delivered from the law, having died to what we were held by, so that we should serve in the newness of the Spirit and not in the oldness of the letter. (Rom. 7:6)

The point is, you can't make yourself righteous by eating from the wrong Tree, and you can't eat from *both* Trees. You will either follow the Spirit or the flesh, *but not both*. To use my illustration, they are opposite ends of the football field.

DIDN'T JESUS SAY HE WASN'T DOING AWAY WITH THE LAW?

Some say that Jesus didn't come to abolish the Law but to fulfill it and that the Law will not pass away until every jot and tittle is fulfilled. That's precisely my point—Jesus DID fulfill every jot and tittle of the Law!

The writer of Hebrews gives us the following:

> When He said, "A new covenant," **He has made the first obsolete.** But whatever is becoming obsolete and growing old is ready to disappear. (Heb. 8:13 NASB)

We know that the New Covenant was established with Jesus' death.[7] The Old did finally "disappear" in 70 AD when all vestiges of keeping the Law and the Temple were destroyed by the Roman armies. Christ fulfilled the Law, thus ending it as a way to live.

This was Paul's point:

> Christ **ended the law** so that everyone who believes in him is made right with God. (Rom. 10:4 ERV)

The word "ended" here is the Greek word *telos*. Thayer's Bible Dictionary defines *telos* as "a termination, an end attained, a consummation; a closing act." [8] The word is most commonly used in the normal definition of "the end."[9] It can also mean the ultimate goal, but either way you look at it, Christ fulfilled the Law's ultimate goal and forever ended it as a way to relate to God.

Our life in Christ is a "new and living way," unprecedented and never before seen or experienced on the earth before Christ.

This is what Paul meant by reminding the mixed up Galatians about our crucified life in Him, "*before whose eyes Jesus Christ was clearly portrayed among you as crucified.*" [10]

There is a popular myth believed by many sincere Bible-believing Christians that the New Covenant is just an extension of the Old Covenant. This is simply not true. Our life in Christ is a "*new and living way,*"[11] unprecedented and *never* before seen or experienced on the earth before Christ. Jesus was the firstborn, the prototype of this new creation.[12]

While the Old Covenant gave us types and shadows, how you walk out grace under the New Covenant is very different than how the people of Israel walked out the Law. The Old Covenant was based on obeying laws, the New Covenant is based on believing promises.

One place where this bewitching mixture of grace and Law comes in is our confusion about the purpose of Jesus' teachings. Jesus' mission was to pull out the roots of the Tree of the Knowledge of Good and Evil from us so we could eat from the Tree of Life—meaning, *only* eat from the Tree of Life.

Jesus, by His teaching, was annihilating the absurd notion that we can do anything to save ourselves or be right with God by human effort and outward behavioral modification. This obliteration made the way for entering into a new way of living as adopted sons under the New Covenant through His death, burial and resurrection.

WHAT'S WRONG WITH THIS TREE?

We know that Adam fell because he ate from the Tree of the Knowledge of Good and Evil in the Garden. But *why* did he eat from its forbidden fruit? While he probably had good intentions, the bottom line is that he wanted to be his own god. We, too, like being our own god. We want to run our own life and also run everyone else's life (by controlling and judging them). The original orphan, Satan, showed us how to live quite well totally separated from the Father's embrace.

It should be easy to understand, then, that even after we come to Christ it still looks "normal" to us to eat from the Tree of the Knowledge of Good and Evil. When we study the Old Testament and see what it looks like for man to try to obey God by eating from this Tree, we think we have our biblical proof text for how we should also live. This is at the heart of all legalism.

However, when we understand that the Old Covenant was God trying to relate to fallen man, who was still eating from the wrong tree, we will begin to understand the reason for the Law. We will also begin to understand our natural hindrance to walking in grace.

As I mentioned in chapter four (Theology Shift), the Father still had to relate to us as immature children until *"the fullness of time had come"* and Christ could reveal His eternal purpose for us to be adopted as sons.

Are you seeing the absurdity of trying to go back to the wrong side of the cross and live by *any part* of the Law yet? The writer of Hebrews said that the Old Covenant was made *obsolete*. That means it's no longer effective.

ARE YOU LIVING BEHIND A FENCE?

Here's another illustration that might help you see what I'm saying. Trying to live by outward behavioral modification and moral restraint is like putting up a fence that puts a boundary between what is acceptable and what is not. This was exactly what the Mosaic Law did.

Even though Jesus delivered us from the Law, we see a perversion of this "fence" in the body of Christ today. It's quite a subjective fence in many churches that are supposedly operating under grace, and I'm sad to say, many of my Charismatic and Pentecostal brethren are some of the worst perpetrators of this legalistic poison.

Traditionally, legalism might look like dress requirements, the right kind of music, acceptable hairstyles, no drinking or smoking, and the rest of the list of what we "don't do." As long as I stay inside this fence of acceptable behavior, I'm okay. If I go outside, I'm condemned. And if I see anyone else go outside this behavioral boundary, I can condemn them, too.

But understand that under the Old Covenant, this was a *lethal fence!* Violating many of the Mosaic Laws resulted in being cut off, stoned…killed. In the books of Leviticus and Numbers alone, the term *"put to death"* is used 25 times (NKJV).

Of course, we don't literally put people to death or stone them anymore. No, here's what we do. After we've decided which sins are acceptable and which ones are not, we now have the right to judge them. We "stone" them by kicking them out, or maybe just by rejecting, labeling, demonizing, withholding forgiveness, back-biting, gossiping, and so forth. After all, they've crossed our fence line of acceptable behavior. If we were playing the game of Tag, they would be "it."

The point is, living behind a fence is not freedom; it's just another form of bondage (a religious one).

Here are a few reasons why living by this subjective fence we've created is not a good idea:

- I will live sin-conscious instead of living God-conscious. My awareness is on the fence, on "not sinning" and trying to manage my behavior (staying inside the fence), not on God.
- It actually hinders me from relying on the Holy Spirit. My focus is on performance instead of abiding in and giving away God's love, which is the only thing that fulfills the Law (Gal. 5:14).
- I will continue living by rules, which separates me from the power of God that actually enables me to live a godly life (Titus 2:11-12), trying in vain to produce fruit that only comes from the Spirit (Gal. 5:22-23).
- I will automatically focus on the behavior of others, those I've deemed to have "crossed over" my subjective behavioral line, comparing myself to them instead of Jesus (2 Cor. 10:12).
- I will want grace for myself but judgment and retribution on others. I will not hold myself accountable for my own behavior. As Jesus pointed out, I automatically become hypocritical and judgmental (Matt. 7:1-5).
- If I'm the one getting caught, I will hide my sin better next time! Just look at our prison system. It may restrain but it cannot transform (Col. 2:20-23).

This is the sad state of the church of behavior modification and sin management. It creates a religious façade that only pushes sin deeper into secret. It fills people with shame and guilt rather than the freedom promised by the gospel.

It seems easier to live by this fence than having to walk by faith toward a God we can't see because we've only learned to trust what we can control and what can be managed in our own strength.

This is why religion uses outward ritual and rules to manage behavior instead of allowing the Holy Spirit to empower us to live a godly life.

Am I advocating living a sinful lifestyle? Absolutely not! I'm advocating trusting God, who is "faithful to complete the work He's begun in me," and will do the same in the lives of others.

The choice is not whether or not to sin, but what motivates our decision: laws and the fear of punishment or the Holy Spirit and love.

I'm advocating Christ and Him crucified *in you*! As Paul had to say after going on and on about this scandalous grace for five chapters in his letter to the Romans—dead people don't need to sin![13]

I'm advocating living inside the Father's love as Jesus lived in His love.[14] What I'm advocating is our being managed by the Holy Spirit instead of by some subjective fence we've created.

I'm also suggesting we trust Him to do whatever work He deems necessary in others. I am saying that we should stop eating from the Tree of the Knowledge of Good and Evil and eat from the Tree of Life. Paul seemed to think that if we walk by the Spirit, we won't fulfill the lusts of the flesh.[15]

This is the "rest" of God and called obedience under the New Covenant. According the writer of Hebrews, this obedience is better than trying to live by outward moral restraint because it was established on better promises.[16]

JESUS OBLITERATED THE FENCE!

The glorious truth of the gospel is that Jesus obliterated our need to live by the fence so that we could live by the supernatural power of the Holy Spirit. Without this fence, there's no more subjective line by which to judge others, no more hypocritical double-standard or self-righteous pretenses. There's no more place for all our legalistic loopholes to make ourselves appear like we're living inside the fence, like the Pharisees in Jesus' day.

Without this fence we *must* live by grace through faith.

What's managing us is the Holy Spirit. But fear not, He's pretty good at it! The New Covenant life means freedom from this lethal fence—freedom from both the rebellious and religious yoke of bondage that Christ died for and staying untangled from it.[17]

The Grace Shift, then, is the transition from being managed by outward rules and moral restraint to being managed by Christ's love empowered to live a godly life through the Holy Spirit.

As I mentioned before, you cannot focus your life in two directions. If you decide to follow the Ten Commandments, you *will* depart from living according to the enabling power of grace by faith. They are at opposite ends of this spectrum.

If you decide to follow the Spirit, you don't need the Ten Commandments. They are fulfilled in the fruit of the Spirit and have already served their purpose—to bring you to Christ:

> Therefore **the law was our tutor to bring us to Christ,** *that we might be justified by faith.* **But after faith has come, we are no longer under a tutor.** (*Gal. 3:24-25*)

Faith *has come!* We're no longer under the Law (Gentiles never were under the Law, by the way). Let's not go back to the religious spiritual orphan life under a tutor, being managed by the "basic principles of the world" and outward rituals, which means we're still eating from the Tree of the Knowledge of Good and Evil that has no effect on the flesh:

> So, then, if with Christ you've **put all that pretentious and infantile religion behind you,** *why do you let yourselves be bullied by it?* **"Don't touch this! Don't taste that! Don't go near this!"** (*Col. 2:20-21 MSG*)
>
> ...*which all concern things which perish with the using—* **according to the commandments and doctrines of**

*men? These things indeed **have an appearance** of wisdom in self-imposed religion, false humility, and neglect of the body, **but are of no value against the indulgence of the flesh.** (Col.2:22-23)*

Beloved, let's put off our "infantile religion" of humanistic struggle against sin that never had the power to transform anyone. God is not taking us back to when He had to relate to us like a small child who needed a tutor, when we didn't have the indwelling Spirit to empower us. The *fullness of time* has come! Christ has revealed the Father as He really is. Christ is now our life, and we are the Father's sons and daughters with His nature.

DOES OUR BEHAVIOR AFFECT OUR SALVATION?

Mary and Pete (not their real names) were having marital issues. Pete decided he'd had enough and started going out to bars, getting involved in shady business deals and eventually cheating on Mary.

Mary was very distraught over Pete's behavior (with good reason) and in the middle of this mess, she said to me in passing, "I just don't want Pete to go to hell."

I stopped and looked at her, "What do you mean by that, Mary?"

"Well, if he keeps this up, he'll lose his soul," she responded.

"So, you're saying that Pete's behavior can affect his salvation?"

"Yes. I guess I am," she said hesitantly.

"Then, what you're saying is that his good behavior got him saved in the first place."

After a few moments of thoughtful silence, Mary looked up and said, "Oh dear, I never thought about it that way!"

What Mary believed was not too different than what many Christians believe about their salvation. This is because we've been taught a grace-law mixed and performance-based gospel message. Of course, we say we're saved by grace, but in reality, we think our bad behavior will send us to hell.

This works great for preachers who thrive on altar calls and manipulating people's guilt and fear. The only problem is…it's not biblical. The truth is, your behavior didn't save you, and your behavior won't send you to hell. You are saved by grace through faith. Period.

So, am I saying that it doesn't' matter what I do? We can just sin all we want?

That isn't what I said.

I said that your sin won't send you to hell. Jesus already dealt with that. You are *already* forgiven, whether you know it or not. But sin will greatly affect you in other very important ways.

SIN DOESN'T COUNT ANYMORE... BUT IT HAS ITS OWN PUNISHMENT

We need to take a look at the way sin is viewed under the New Covenant of grace. What I'm about to say will probably stretch you, maybe even offend your mind because our popular version of Christianity is so steeped in this sin paradigm, but be at peace. What the heart believes usually offends the mind at first.

> And no one, having drunk old wine, immediately desires new; for he says, 'The old is better.'" (Luke 5:39)

As my friend, Mark Hendrickson asks, imagine what it would be like not having to think about or expend energy on sin management, where your thoughts would be free to commune with God. How would you feel? What would your life be like? How would you respond to other people? Imagine never having to waste time hiding from God.

The sad fact is, many sincere believers only "feel" God when they're convicted of their sins.

The sad fact is, many sincere believers only "feel" God when they're convicted of their sins. They call this revival. But conviction of sin is an entry-level God encounter and not at all how He intended for us to live.

The astounding truth is sin doesn't separate us from Him anymore; it creates an *illusion* of separation from Him. What do I mean by this? First, let me clarify what I *don't* mean, along with what I do mean...

- I don't mean that grace gives us license to sin; it empowers us to live in the newness of God's life (Rom. 6:1-7; Titus 2:11-12).
- I don't mean that our behavior doesn't matter; it's a question of who is managing our behavior—us or the Holy Spirit?
- I don't mean that we don't sin anymore. I'm talking about sin's relationship to us and with God.
- I DO mean that the "separating" effect of sin, for God, has been completely taken out of the picture by Jesus on the cross.
- I DO agree with the Father that Jesus' blood was enough!
- I DO agree that it is finished!

And that, my friend, is GOOD news. Jesus dealt with *all* sin on the cross—past, present, and future—and ALL your sins were in the future when He accomplished this. Which means, He can't be dealing with them now because He was crucified *once for all*. Here's what the writer of Hebrews says about it:

> *Their sins and lawless acts* **I will remember no more."**
> *And where these have been forgiven, sacrifice for sin is* **no longer necessary.** *(Heb. 10:17-18 NIV)*

Paul said it this way...

> *...God was reconciling the world to himself in Christ,* **not counting people's sins against them.** *(2 Cor. 5:19 NIV)*

The only thing we can conclude here is that sin is not remembered by God, and that He's not counting our sin against us.

Do we actually believe this?

The only truthful thing we can do is agree and say (confess, declare) the same thing as God. Jesus' sacrifice took away *all* of our sins. All means all! They *were* forgiven and forgotten forever. Our only part is to receive this glorious gift of forgiveness and deliverance by faith and say, thank You!

This is true repentance; we're no longer trying to save ourselves by religious self-effort but accepting His salvation by grace through faith. This is the most amazing thing about grace. Sin is not an issue between us and God.

Yet, many blood-bought Christians don't believe this. Furthermore, not only do they think God is remembering and counting their sins against them, they're remembering and counting everybody else's sins against them, too! This legalistic view of sin always makes us judgmental and divisive. The irony is quite astounding in light of the fact that declaring God's complete forgiveness and reconciliation *is our ministry*.

> *Now all things are of God, who has* **reconciled us** *to Himself through Jesus Christ, and* **has given us the ministry of reconciliation** *(2 Cor. 5:18)*

Not that God needs to be reconciled to us, but He is pleading for us to be reconciled to Him!

> *Now then, we are ambassadors for Christ,* **as though God were pleading through us:** *we implore you on Christ's behalf,* **be reconciled to God.** *(2 Cor. 5:20)*

This is New Covenant evangelism. God is not counting your sins against you anymore. Put down your rocks and be reconciled!

Back to the question I asked earlier: Does this mean that I can now just go do whatever I want and sin to my heart's content with no consequences? Hallelujah, thank you Jesus?

Uh…no…

That is, technically, you could, but only if you wanted to live a toxic life full of defeat, bondage, fear, confusion, woundedness, regret, disappointment, addiction, broken relationships, and lots of other garbage piled up in your life that God never intended you to have.

Here's what Paul said about this.

> *"We are allowed to do anything," so they say. That is true, but not everything is good. We are allowed to do anything—but not everything is helpful. (1 Cor. 10:23 GNT)*

He said something similar earlier in the same letter (1 Cor. 6:12). The spiritually immature and divisive Corinthians were apparently taking Paul's scandalous message of grace in two ways. On one hand, people were apparently using grace as an excuse to live a sinful lifestyle. On the other, his accusers were pointing to Paul's radical, sloppy-agape, hyper-grace message as the reason for their moral departure (nothing new there).

This irony is quite astounding in light of the fact that declaring God's complete forgiveness and reconciliation is our ministry.

Paul's response to these accusations is quite shocking, especially to religious people still living by the "fence" instead of by the Spirit. If you're still living according to this outwardly moral fence, it will shock you, too.

He totally agreed with their accusations!

He did say that everything was legal for a Christian to do. We were already completely forgiven at the cross—past, present, and future.

Sin *cannot* separate us from God. The Father is pretty happy with Jesus' sacrifice and seems to think it's finished forever. But Paul's point was that it wasn't in our best interest to do sinful things because they would affect the joy and love we have in Christ.

Sin doesn't separate God from us, *it creates an illusion of separation between us and Him.* It clouds *our side* of our relationship with God because we're still believing these alien identities that Satan and other people have given us.

To put it succinctly, sin is bondage.

Since Paul clearly saw sin as a toxic poison instead of forbidden fruit, why would he ever want to do those things? It would be like me saying that while it's technically legal to eat rat poison, it would be very foolish and harmful to do so, even deadly. Yes, I am still loved and accepted by my family, by God if I do, but why would I want to poison myself?

Paul was saying it would not be "helpful" to do anything that would put him back into the bondage from which Christ set him free. We, too, should understand this truth.

Living empowered by grace means that if every sinful thing in this world were completely legal and somehow morally okay for me to do, I still would not engage in anything that would hinder love and my ongoing conscious awareness of God's presence in my life.

I would not do anything that would put me back into bondage. This was Paul's point. Do you see this yet?

When Christians sin, they are doing so out of ignorance of this reality. Their mind has not yet been transformed to where they now see sin as a toxic poison instead of forbidden fruit.

> *Since Paul clearly saw sin as a toxic poison instead of forbidden fruit, why would he ever want to do those things?*

Grace does what the Law and outward moral restraint could never do. The Law made sin a forbidden fruit and, thus, *heightened* our awareness of sin.[18] God's grace is the only thing that can truly restrain us from sinful behavior because it transforms our heart's desire to only want what's best for us. And what's best for us is exactly what God wants for us. We're not like Adam in the Garden, thinking God is holding out on us. Grace has opened our eyes to the Tree of Life. We now understand that the counterfeit pleasures of sin cannot hold a candle to the infinite joy and pleasure found in His embrace.

So, yes, under the New Covenant, we *can* do *anything* we want. We are saved by grace through faith *alone,* not by our behavior. Which also means our behavior cannot send us to hell. But it doesn't mean that what we're doing is good for us. In fact, it could be very harmful.

The tragedy of believers pursuing a sinful lifestyle is not that they plunge themselves headlong into the eternal flames, it's that they never let the Holy Spirit show them what's inside of them that's broken. When we keep blaming our spouse, other people, or our circumstances, we never let God show us what's going on in our own soul. We never become fully who we were created to be. We stay broken.

As Paul emphatically stated, the Law is for law-breakers, not for God's beloved sons and daughters living by grace through faith. This is why laws are needed in civil society.

> *We know that the law is good when used correctly. For the law was not intended for people who do what is right. It is for people who are lawless and rebellious.... (1 Tim. 1:8-9 NLT)*

> *The tragedy of believers pursuing a sinful lifestyle is ...that they never let the Holy Spirit show them what's inside of them that's broken.*

The conclusion? Jesus already took sin away from God's side of the equation. Everyone is *already* forgiven, it's a free gift received by faith alone. We can be as stupid as we want, live in a cesspool if we want. God will never love us any more or any less. Nothing will ever change on His end. But sin *does* matter on my end, for it has its own punishment by the toll it takes on my life.

This finished fact of forgiveness cannot change because the covenant was already fulfilled between Jesus and the Father at the cross.[19] We didn't make this Covenant so we can't break it. We can only agree with it and walk in its power to change us.

GRACE IS ABOUT TRUE FREEDOM

The purpose of God's grace is not primarily about escaping punishment. It's about empowering freedom. God wants you to be free just as He is free.

Our problem is we've only known various forms of bondage we thought were freedom. God must take us through a process to help us understand that His freedom is better than our freedom. This process is the renewing of our mind.[20] He wants us to see things the way He sees them. It should take no stretch of faith for us to believe that His understanding of joy and life and freedom is infinitely better than ours.

What is this grace freedom all about then?

It's God's life within you that empowers you to fully function in all you were meant to be. As Graham Cooke said at a leadership conference I attended recently, *"Grace is the empowering presence of God that enables you to become the person that He sees when He looks at you."*

"Grace is the empowering presence of God that enables you to become the person that He sees when He looks at you."
Graham Cooke

When we properly understand this, we find that God's grace is boundless, just as His love is unfathomable and His joy is infinite.

Grace is more about empowering who God made you to be in Christ rather than about getting what you don't deserve. I realize that this is a different take than you've always heard but, again, only because of the deeply entrenched sin-conscious paradigm we've had in our culture for centuries. While I do agree that everything we receive from God is unmerited, it still misses the main point of grace.

Defining grace simply as unmerited favor also means that Jesus cannot be our example of what it looks like to walk in grace. As Graham Cooke has also pointed out, *"If grace is the unmerited favor of God, then Jesus didn't have any."* Yet, Jesus was full of grace and truth.

The sin issue for us on *this side* of the cross is not a question of being right with God. As we already saw, we can only be right with God by faith. The real issue is when we still don't see that sin has its own punishment in the form of the bondage and toll it takes on our lives.

Claiming grace to get away with wrong doing is the baby end of Christian living. As C.S. Lewis said, it's wanting to make mud pies in a slum when a holiday by the sea is offered to us.[21]

Sin is bondage and slavery, and we are no longer to be slaves. It's not appropriate because we died and our life is Christ's life. Spiritual maturity is finding the source of our life from Christ. Everything we do from this place in Him will be filled with His joy and love.

We're not freed to sin; we're freed from sin's power to enslave us. Grace has opened our eyes to what the fruit of the Knowledge of Good and Evil actually is, and now we're eating freely from the Tree of Life. Sin no longer defines us, empowers our heart, nor does it begin to compare with the immeasurable power and "fullness that fills God" that works within us.[22] There's really no contest. I will finish this chapter with my favorite passage from the Message Bible:

> *Dear, dear Corinthians, I can't tell you how much I long for you* **to enter this wide open, spacious life.** *We didn't fence you in.* **The smallness you feel comes from within you.** *Your lives aren't small, but you're living them in a small way. I'm speaking as plainly as I can and with great affection. Open up your lives.* **Live openly and expansively!** *(2 Cor. 6:12-13)*

Hear what the Spirit is saying here. Live your life openly and expansively. Don't let the "smallness" of grace-law mixture of orphan-hearted religion or rebellion fence you in.

You are free as God is free. Live in His boundless life of grace. It's more amazing than you can possibly imagine.

CHAPTER SEVEN ENDNOTES

---

[1] See Galatians 1:6-9; 3:1-5

[2] See 2 Corinthians 5:14-16; Galatians 5:22-23

[3] I gave a basic definition and outline of the mindset of a spiritual orphan in the first chapter titled, "What is Son Shift?"

[4] Jim McNeely III, *The Romance of Grace*, Libertary (2013), chapter six

[5] See Ephesians 3:20; 2 Peter 1:4

[6] Luke 15:31

[7] See Romans 7:4-6

[8] Thayer's Expanded Greek Definition, Electronic Database. Copyright © 2002, 2003, 2006, 2011 by Biblesoft, Inc. All rights reserved. Used by permission.

[9] See Matthew 10:22; 24:6, 13, 14; Luke 1:33; John 13:1; 1 Corinthians 1:8; 10:11; 15:24; Philippians 3:19; Hebrews 3:14; Revelation 21:6; 22:13

[10] See Galatians 3:1

[11] See Hebrews 10:20

[12] See Colossians 1:15

[13] See Romans 6:1-2

[14] See John 15:19-11

[15] See Galatians 5:16

[16] See Hebrews 8:6

[17] See Galatians 5:1

[18] See Romans 7:5-8

[19] See Galatians 3:15-17

[20] See Romans 12:2

[21] C.S. Lewis, *The Weight of Glory*, HarperCollins (2001), 26

[22] See Ephesians 3:19-20

FAITH SHIFT

For we walk by faith, not by sight. – 2 Corinthians 5:7

"What do you do that an atheist can't do?"

This question was God's opening to a conversation I had with Him several years back. Did you ever notice that whenever God asks you a question, He's not looking for information? I've learned that it's usually the beginning of revelation…for me. And I was about to get a big one.

Now, I didn't perceive any rebuke or condemning tone in the voice. It was more that of a gentle loving father. But He had my attention. At this point in my ignorance, I was sure there was plenty that I could do that an atheist couldn't do. Of course, I was about to have my world turned upside down. Here's essentially how this conversation went…

"What do you do that an atheist can't do?" I heard from the Voice.

"I can preach. I countered…

"Atheists can motivate people too," came the inaudible reply.

"I can teach the Bible."

"So could they if they studied it and were trained to do so."

"We have very moving times of worship during our services."

"There are talented atheist musicians and songwriters who can move people's hearts, even to tears."

"I can give good counsel."

"So can their psychologists and counselors."

"I can give people principles for a better life."

"So can they...."

"We have stronger families and marriages."

(No response)

Then I remembered reading a study where it was found that atheists have a better track record in successful marriages than Christians[1] ...that was depressing.

At this point, I was getting the basic idea of what God was driving at...

"Okay, I give up. I guess there isn't much that I can do, nor is there much that we do in our church services, that atheists can't do."

The only sure thing I knew I had over the atheist was that I believed I was going to heaven when I died; they don't. Of course, they don't care either.

God had me right where He wanted me—ready to receive revelation. The revelation was two-fold. First, there are many things that Christians can do that atheists can't do, but *all* of them *require* faith and are usually a demonstration of the supernatural power of God. The second revelation was personal and hard to take. I realized that I was what Bill Johnson has referred to as an *unbelieving believer.*

I was stunned.

Here I was, a so-called "Bible-believing" Christian for almost 30 years at this time. I was no Cessationist[2] but a Charismatic pastor, fully convinced that the gifts of the Spirit and everything in the Bible is for today. I had many personal encounters with God. Suddenly I was realizing that I had bought into a brand of Christianity that wasn't much different than being a well-behaved and educated atheist.

Oh yes, I *agreed* that all of the word of God was inspired and 100% truth; I just didn't really believe it. You see, you only truly believe what you practice. This was James' point.[3] And I didn't practice most of what it said I could do in Christ. Apparently I practiced only the things that atheists could also practice in their own power.

Very little of my activities or the activities of my church resembled anything I saw Jesus doing or the church doing in the book of Acts, nor did I have the same world-changing effect on my culture that they had.

Our so-called "Spirit-filled" services were still very predictable and at a very human level. Oh, we had great worship, occasional prophecy, tongues and the usual Charismatic fare.

> *I agreed that all of the word of God was inspired and 100% truth; I just didn't really believe it.*

Nonetheless, we had essentially the same relational squabbles and problems that unbelievers in the world have. We faced the circumstances and issues of our everyday life just like unbelievers did…on a human level. We had the same limited and powerless mindset as they have in just about everything.

The crazy thing was we thought that was normal! I hadn't seen that Paul actually rebuked the earthbound Corinthians for acting like *mere human beings*.[4] So much for "only being human" as an excuse.

Jesus' life and ministry was not my standard for Christian living and ministry. My culture and what other churches were doing were my standards. As Jonathan Welton points out in his book, *Normal Christianity*,[5] I was an average Christian instead of a normal Christian. (Jesus being the standard for a "normal" Christian.)

I finally saw what we did and valued in our version of Christianity was not what Jesus and the New Testament writers did and valued. Their version of *"doing good"* was healing the sick, casting out demons, and raising the dead. We trust more in taking medicine, practicing psychology, and having funerals to deal with those kinds of things. We value knowledge, seminary degrees, charismatic personalities, good looks, eloquent preaching, programs, and scholarly teaching.

I'm not at all saying that any of these things are bad in and of themselves. I believe it's a blessing from God to have access to advanced technology and medical science. Hey, at least doctors are trying to heal people, and they do a great job. But we have Christians saying it's God's will that they have some disease and not get healed. How absurd is that!

Do we fail to see that Paul trusted in and valued something very different? He actually rejected his religious scholarship and circumstantial living in favor of living a supernatural life in Christ and walking in Holy Spirit revelation.[6] Paul wanted his Spirit-filled but worldly Corinthians to trust in something totally other worldly.

> *And my speech and my preaching were **not with persuasive words** of human wisdom, **but in demonstration of the Spirit and of power**, that your faith **should not be in** the wisdom of men but in **the power of God**. (2 Cor. 2:4-5)*

Do you see that? Paul wanted them to actually put their faith in the supernatural power of God more than in clever preaching! We do the opposite. We value and trust persuasive words and are suspicious of supernatural power. We're no show and all tell. We want to argue people into the Kingdom rather than demonstrate it for them.

Jesus seemed to think that believers will lay hands on sick and they will recover.[7] Apparently, unbelieving believers don't. I know I didn't. We made up things like, "That's for special people with a special healing gift." My powerless prayers amounted to begging God to do something He told me to do. I said "amen" to the *theory* of "Christ in me" and being seated in heavenly places, but I acted like He was "up there" and I was "down here."

I lived like a spiritual orphan, waiting for Papa to come home. Like the elder brother, waiting until I died for the things He said I already had available to me.[8] I certainly didn't believe that I could raise the dead! But Jesus seemed to think I should do all of these things in the normal course of ministry, and even greater things.[9]

My faith was humanistic, based on what I could understand with my intellect and do naturally. The Kingdom of God coming to earth was something that would only happen when Jesus returned.

So, with this encounter with God, my small and powerless Christian world was being rocked at its very foundation.

> *"Cultural longevity legitimatizes absurdity."*
> Sam Soleyn

I saw that my "faith" was based on my circumstances, not by what God actually says in His Word. I realized I had changed what He said about me and how I was supposed to live into something compatible with my cultural surroundings. It's cultural because we don't really believe in miracles, signs, and wonders as a matter of course in our rational Western churches even though these are happening with regularity through very common people in other parts of the world.

The problem with cultural influence is if you say something long enough, and it *sounds* biblical, it becomes the culture's orthodoxy. As Sam Soleyn points out, *"Cultural longevity legitimatizes absurdity."* [10]

We have inherited several centuries of humanistic-based deistic[11] Christianity that teaches us a lot of good things but denies the miraculous and supernatural (unless it's to say the devil is doing it), which makes our "Churchianity" look more like Greek philosophy than Kingdom reality.

Of course, we can just dismiss and demonize people who dare to believe what the Bible calls "normal" as hyper and extreme—a false gospel. I saw myself for what I really was, and I was shocked. I laugh at the utter irony of it all when I think about it now.

GETTING OUT OF THE BOAT OF MY COMFORTABLE UNBELIEF

So this paradigm-changing revelation of my unbelief was the *beginning* of faith for me. Since this encounter, I've been contending for a lifestyle of faith, learning from the best who walk in this supernatural Kingdom reality and learning how to do what I see my Father do.[12]

We walk by faith, not fatalism.

I have seen hundreds of people healed, many on death's door, many miraculously healed of incurable diseases. I have seen financial miracles in my own life and in the life of others, and hopeless marriages restored. I have seen people miraculously set free from all kinds of demonic strongholds, and best of all, I have had many love encounters with my heavenly Papa as I learn how to rest in His embrace.

I have also expected miracles that never came. I have had people literally die in my hands as I was praying for their recovery. Nonetheless, many are living now who would not be, because we risked taking God at His word. I am growing in all of this.

I still see too much sadness and not enough joy and victory, but that doesn't change what I believe to be true. I'm never going back to my old safe but powerless "unbelieving" version of Christianity again. It's too late for that. I'm determined for Jesus to get His full reward in and through me. I will live in the tension of believing what I cannot see even when what I do see seems to totally contradict it.

As John Wimber[13] used to say, "Faith is spelled, "R-I-S-K." That means getting out of my comfortable boat of unbelief and learning how to walk on the water with Jesus until my experience matches what He believes about me.

FAITH ACCESSES THE PROMISES OF GOD

You were not saved by grace. You were saved by grace *through faith*.[14] Faith is how we access the promises of God and the transforming power of His grace.

The writer of Hebrews said that the children of Israel, who were miraculously delivered out of Egypt, heard the gospel but still died in the wilderness because they didn't mix the promise with faith.[15]

The truth is *all* the promises of God are "yes and amen" to you in Christ,[16] but they're like wrapped presents under a Christmas tree. They're already yours, but they will remain unopened and useless until you receive those promises. Faith is the key to unlocking the promises of God. We walk by faith, not fatalism.

Jesus was pretty clear that faith works like a self-fulfilling prophecy. Like He told the Centurion, *as we believe*, it will done for us.[17] The opposite is also true. For instance, if you don't believe in healing, you probably won't be seeing many people getting healed. If you think you're just a "dirty sinner," you will pretty much act like one.

As Bill Johnson has said, *"the person who believes they're a 'sinner saved by grace' sins by faith."*

The Faith Shift we need to make, then, is moving from "seeing is believing" to "believing is seeing." It's transitioning from seeing our current experience as reality to seeing what God says as more real than our current experience.

This Faith Shift begins when you not only believe *in* Jesus, but begin to believe *like* Jesus, for we have the "mind of Christ."[18] This is the very essence of having our mind renewed.

My experience has been that most Christians don't have "faith toward God,"[19] they have faith toward their circumstances. Rather than believing what God says about them; they wait to see if what He said will actually work in their lives before they will commit to it. This is the opposite of biblical faith. Sadly, faith was circumstantial for most of my Christian life.

Faith Shift happens when we stop basing what we believe on what we *can* believe according to our human limitations. It's when we start getting out of our safe "boat" and walking onto the uncertain sea and actually trust that Jesus won't let us drown.[20]

IS IT FAITH WHEN WE *CAN* SEE?

We preach a lot of sermons, write books, and sing Christian songs about walking by faith. We act like "normal faith" is living by our circumstances, but when times get really tough there's a "special" walking by faith for *even when I cannot see*. But believing God over our circumstances is the only faith there is!

For we walk by faith, not by sight. (2 Cor. 5:7)

A careful look at this verse tells us that walking by what we can see and faith are mutually exclusive. In other words, when you can see a thing, it doesn't require *any faith at all*, yet we seem to have adopted this absurd view of faith. It isn't actually faith, but we think it is.

We have a choice to make. Either we will believe only what we see, or we will believe what we don't see but what God says is true. Considering there is a whole lot going on that we cannot see, even in creation, we could be missing a lot by making the wrong choice.

I will simply put it to you this way: is what we can see all there is to reality? Up until the latter part of the nineteenth century, medical science didn't believe in germs and bacteria because they couldn't see them and many people died. More recently, discoveries in quantum physics seem to reveal that there are at least eleven dimensions, probably more. These dimensions aren't just very small like germs, they're not even in the time-space realm at all!

So, if we cannot even comprehend most of physical creation by natural means, how are we going to grasp the greater spiritual reality without faith? Yet, the eyes of faith *do* see these things, as the writer of Hebrews points out:

> *By faith we understand that the worlds were framed by the*
> *word of God, so that the things which are seen were not*
> *made of things which are visible. (Heb. 11:3)*

FAITH THAT TRANSFORMS YOUR EXPERIENCE

I mentioned at the beginning of this chapter that most people trust in their experience more than what God says about them in His Word. This is the opposite of faith toward God. When we finally decide to bring our current experience up to what God's Word says about us instead of dumbing down what His Word says to our experience, we will begin the transformation process.

Now let's see how this Faith Shift works. Simply put, it comes by applying our faith in the *opposite direction* of what we're used to doing. Understand, we *all* have faith in something. Even atheists have faith. Doubt is just having more faith in other things. Having faith is not the issue, it's *where* we apply our faith that's the issue. Let me explain what I mean with the help of someone who was very influential in my understanding of faith.

Watchman Nee was an early twentieth century Chinese Christian teacher who had profound revelation of these things. I encourage you read his classic works, *The Normal Christian Life* and *Living the Overcoming Life*. In the second book, he talks about the process of experientially "growing up into Christ."[21] We can see how this Faith Shift works by using this simple three-word diagram:

FACT ← FAITH → EXPERIENCE

Basically, it works like this. The facts are what God says about you in His word. For instance, He says you're crucified with Christ, totally forgiven and dead to sin, seated with Him in heavenly places. You are complete in Him, with *His* righteousness and holiness. Jesus says you will do what He did and greater things. Actually, the Bible says that as

He is, so are you in this world.

You may be thinking your current experience doesn't seem to line up with His facts at all. In fact, most of your life seems to be in contradiction to who God says you are in His Word.

Here is what we do. We apply our faith to His facts (arrow going to the left in the diagram). In other words, we look at *God's* assessment of us rather than what our circumstances are trying to tell us. When we do this, the Holy Spirit will bring revelation knowledge, which transports His facts into our experience.

As we receive more revelation by faith, our experience will begin to line up with what God says about us.

This is how transformation takes place. As we receive more revelation by faith, our experience will begin to line up with what God says about us. In other words, applying faith to His facts leads to spiritual *revelation*, which leads to *transformation*. This transformation leads to *incarnation*, which is where our lives are now coming into sync with who we already are in Christ.

This process is called renewing your mind.[22] It doesn't happen all at once, but if you keep doing this—applying faith to God's facts—your experience will begin to line up with these facts.

Unfortunately, "unbelieving believers" tend to put their faith in their current experience (arrow going toward the right in the diagram). They look away from God's facts and toward what they're circumstances are telling them.

As in the example I used before, when we say that we will believe (faith) that God still heals (fact) only when we see someone get healed (experience), the Bible calls this unbelief. Can you see that this is applying our faith in the wrong direction? We're actually going in the direction of unbelief. We're applying faith to our experience instead of God's facts, so His Word becomes more like a fairytale to us. This inevitably dumbs God's Word down to our experience. We've put God in the box of our limited ability to understand.

Applying our faith to our circumstances and what people tell us is how we lived before we came to Christ. This is the "old man" that Paul tells us to put off.[23] We do this by faith.

FAITH HAS ITS FOUNDATION IN THE PAST

Everything about faith has its anchor in the past. It was accomplished on the cross 2,000 years ago. This is very good news because it also means that it cannot be undone.

Furthermore, every promise and everything you are to believe about yourself in Christ is already done. You cannot make it happen; it *already* happened.

You can only believe it or not believe it.

There are three historical facts of faith. We've already covered some of this in other chapters but will summarize here.

1. We were healed by His beating. The first thing we need to see is that Jesus was beaten before He went to the cross so that we would be healed–physically, spiritually, and emotionally. This means that all sickness and disease and oppression were dealt with when Christ was beaten on the whipping post.

The prophet Isaiah looks forward to this event, Peter looks backward…

*And by His stripes we **are** healed.... (Isa. 53:5)*

*...by whose stripes you **were** healed. (1 Pet. 2:24)*

There is controversy in the body of Christ over what type of healing is in the atonement, but there really shouldn't be. Matthew gives us the divine commentary on what Isaiah meant. We clearly see deliverance from demonic oppression and physical healing in view here:

When evening had come, they brought to Him many who

*were demon-possessed. And **He cast out the spirits with a word, and healed all who were sick**, that it might be fulfilled which was **spoken by Isaiah the prophet**, saying: He Himself **took our infirmities** and **bore our sicknesses**. (Matt. 8:16-17; cf. Isa. 53:4)*

We appropriate this historical fact by faith in His name. In this case, the name *Adonai Rapha* – "Lord, our healer."[24]

2. We were completely forgiven—forever—by Jesus' blood. The second wonderful historical fact is that Jesus' blood shed on the cross was for complete forgiveness for ALL mankind,[25] and we've been cleansed from ALL sin.[26] This means *all* sin—past, present and future. As we already saw in the last chapter, Hebrews tells us that He did it once and for all—forever.[27] Because of Christ's sacrifice, God is not holding our sins against us anymore.[28] Do you believe this?

Now, God is dealing with our new nature. It's about forming Christ in us.[29] Paul says later, it's not about outward ritual or any other form of sin-management, it's about a new creation.[30]

Welcome to the New Covenant!

The sad fact is even though every human being has God's complete forgiveness for their sins, many will not receive this free gift. They will go into eternity separating *themselves* from God, even though they've been totally forgiven.

Another sad fact is that too many Christians live bound up in condemnation and shame because they think God is angry with them about their sins.

3. Our sinful nature was nailed to the cross. The third wonderful historical fact of Christ's atoning work is that our sinful nature was nailed to the Cross.[31] As we saw in chapter six (Identity Shift), our problem is not that we don't understand Jesus' death, burial, and resurrection. It's that we don't identify *ourselves* as dead, buried, and resurrected with Him.

Paul seems to think that your past is gone:

*This means that anyone who belongs to Christ has become a new person. **The old life is gone**; a new life has begun! (2 Cor. 5:17 NLT)*

Our Adamic nature *was* crucified with Christ! What we still have are sin habits and an unrenewed mind.

Finally, we must understand that the Bible sees these three aspects of the atonement inextricably linked together. In other words, you cannot biblically separate healing from forgiveness of sin or the death of your old nature. Here's how Peter tied them together. Notice that all three wonderful facts are past tense:

*who Himself **bore our sins** in His own body on the tree, that we, **having died** to sins, might live for righteousness—by whose stripes you **were healed**. (1 Pet. 2:24)*

ALL of these wonderful promises are available to you and waiting to be accessed by faith. The psalmist sums it up beautifully, telling us not to forget *any* of these benefits available to us:

Bless the Lord, O my soul, and forget not all His benefits: Who forgives all your iniquities, Who heals all your diseases, Who redeems your life from destruction, Who crowns you with lovingkindness and tender mercies, Who satisfies your mouth with good things, so that your youth is renewed like the eagle's. (Psalm 103:2-5)

Again, do you actually believe this?

It doesn't matter what your experience has been telling you; put off the old way of thinking and look to Christ with eyes of faith!

What do you need today? Freedom from guilt and shame? Some physical or emotional healing? Deliverance from oppression? Fulfillment? Renewal? Don't empower what Jesus has disempowered on the cross another day. Believe the promises. It's already done in Christ!

LIVING BY FAITH IN THE FATHER'S EMBRACE

We've been looking at how faith transforms our experience by believing what God says about us, but our discussion would not be complete without taking into consideration how we exercise faith when we don't know God's will about something. Maybe it's a decision we need to make, we don't know the timing, or the Bible doesn't clearly define it for us. We find these answers in how Jesus lived in His Father's embrace.

Jesus said, *"The Son can do nothing of Himself, but what He sees the Father do; for whatever He does, the Son also does in like manner."* His faith was forged and refined through intimacy and submission to His Father's will.

Hebrews 11 starts out by saying, "Faith is the SUBSTANCE of things hoped for…." Furthermore, "faith comes by HEARING" and hearing by the word (*rhema*) of God.[32] *Rhema* is the Greek word used here. It means the "word" God speaks to our heart.

Faith, then, is a concrete substance that comes by hearing God's voice. Since His sheep are to know His voice and know His character, then when we hear His voice, it produces substance, which produces a confident assurance of success for whatever is before us. This is how we walk by faith in all things!

I highly recommend that you check out Mark Hendrickson's blog post titled "Fleece Template" that can help you find the will of God in your decision making.[33]

Beloved, we must make this Faith Shift. This world we've been called to is too broken, too crippled, too sick, too hopeless, and too bound by Satan's lies and bondages for us to stay in our powerless, humanistic version of Christianity. We cannot let the enemy destroy the very ones Jesus came to make free.

It really *does* matter what we believe.

CHAPTER EIGHT ENDNOTES

[1] This comes from research from the Barna Group. The original study is no longer online, but is included in an article titled, "U.S. divorce rates for various faith groups, age groups, & geographic areas" found at: http://www.religioustolerance.org/chr_dira.htm

[2] Cessationism is the belief that the supernatural gifts of the Holy Spirit ended with the apostles.

[3] See James 2:14-26

[4] 1 Corinthians 3:3 NIV

[5] Jonathan Welton, *Normal Christianity: If Jesus is Normal, What is the Church?*, Destiny Image (2011)

[6] See Philippians 3:4-8

[7] Mark 16:16-17

[8] Luke 15:31

[9] John 14:12

[10] Sam Soleyn, www.soleyn.com

[11] Deism is the belief in the existence of a God on the evidence of reason and nature only, with rejection of supernatural revelation.

[12] John 5:19; 20:21

[13] John Wimber was a founder of the Vineyard movement

[14] Ephesians 2:8a *"For by grace you have been saved through faith..."*

[15] See Hebrews 4:2

[16] See 2 Corinthians 1:20

[17] Matthew 8:13

[18] See 1 Corinthians 2:16

[19] See Hebrews 6:1

[20] See Matthew 14:25-32

[21] See Ephesians 4:15

[22] See Romans 12:1-2; 2 Corinthians 10:3-5

[23] See Romans 6:6; Ephesians 4:22

[24] See Exodus 15:22-26

[25] See 1 John 2:2

[26] See Ephesians 1:7; Colossians 1:14

[27] See Hebrews 10:12

[28] See 2 Corinthians 5:19

[29] See Galatians 4:19; Ephesians 4:15

[30] See Galatians 6:15

[31] See Romans 6:6-7; Colossians 2:13-14

[32] Romans 10:17

[33] Mark Hendrickson's post, "Fleece template" found at: http://wp.me/p23r7p-3r

HEAVEN SHIFT

"And they lived happily ever after."

Heaven, for most people, seems to be about a happy ending. I think that's why most fairytales end with one.

During the Medieval period, brave knights would be promised heaven if they fought in the Crusades. Today, there are religious zealots who will strap bombs on their chest to ensure a place in heaven.

Some people believe that heaven is a fairytale, but everybody who believes in heaven wants to go there when they die. This is what makes following statement of Jesus in Luke so interesting:

> *Now when He was asked by the Pharisees when the king-dom of God would come, He answered them and said, "The kingdom of God does not come with observation; nor will they say, 'See here!' or 'See there!' For indeed, **the kingdom of God is within you.** (Luke 17:20-21)*

Jesus is basically turning the whole idea of heaven and the kingdom of God on its head by saying that it's within you. That's what I call a Heaven Shift!

For centuries, Christians have been living as though heaven is "up there" in the sky somewhere and we're down here on earth. This wasn't far from the truth under the Old Covenant. Solomon said, *"For God is in heaven, and you on earth."*[1] Case closed, right?

Well, no, because everything changed with Jesus.

The very first thing Jesus announced when He started His ministry was that the kingdom of God was now within our reach.[2] We will see that He said this because He brought heaven with Him. Paul also tells us we are seated in heavenly places in Christ.

But up until a few years ago, I was like Solomon and most Christians I knew. I didn't live like I was seated in heavenly places at all. I was still waiting for something else.

> *Jesus is basically turning the whole idea of heaven and the kingdom of God on its head by saying that it's within you.*

Most Christians believe that Jesus brought the Kingdom with Him. The problem is, they also seem to think He took it back with Him when He left! Jesus was here, now He's gone. The Kingdom was here, now it's gone away with Jesus. So now we're waiting for the Kingdom to return when He returns.

However, this misses the whole point of Jesus coming in the first place. Jesus came in human flesh so we could be with Him in heavenly places, now *and* forever!

Certainly, heaven will come in greater fullness with the physical return of Christ, but when He left, He gave us the Holy Spirit to bring the Kingdom of heaven to the earth like He did.

So the Heaven Shift we need to make is about this change in perspective. In other words, it's about changing our traditional perspective of living from earth to heaven to one where we're seeing ourselves living from heaven to earth. I will explain what I mean by this as we go.

For now, just know this shift can change everything about the way you see yourself in Christ, and everything else for that matter.

MY PERSONAL HEAVEN SHIFT

Several years ago, I decided to read Bill Johnson's book, *When Heaven Invades Earth*. On one particular evening I was reading what he wrote about Jacob's dream.[3] Most Christians know the story well. It's about a dream Jacob had with angels going up and down a ladder into heaven. It's also the first mention of the "house of God" in the Bible. I knew that whenever God mentions something the first time in Scripture, you want to pay close attention because it shows the DNA, or original intent, for that particular term or concept.

In this case, He is showing something about His purpose for His people, the Church, which is the "house of God." What Johnson said inspired me so I got my Bible out and here's what I read:

> *"Now Jacob went out from Beersheba and went toward Haran. So he came to a certain place and stayed there all night, because the sun had set. And he took one of the stones of that place and put it at his head, and he lay down in that place to sleep. Then he dreamed, and behold, a ladder was set up on the earth, and its top reached to heaven; and there the angels of God were ascending and descending on it....Behold, I am with you and will keep you wherever you go... Then Jacob awoke from his sleep and said, "Surely the LORD is in this place, and I did not know it." And he was afraid and said, "How awesome is this place!* **This is none other than the house of God, and this is the gate of heaven!**" *(Gen. 28:10-12, 15-17)*

As I'm reading this passage, I'm getting what I can only describe as an out of body experience! I'd never had one before so I wasn't sure if it was one, but it was like I was moving away from my body, suspended above the page and I could hear God saying in my mind, *"Pay attention...I'm going to show you something that is going to change your world!"*

The instant anticipation this created was tremendous. And it did change my world, to say the least!

I heard Him say, *"You are called to be a "Gate Church" for your surrounding area."*

Please understand, I didn't take this to mean that our local church was any better than any other church. In fact, as I studied this out later, I found that *all* local churches are called to be "Gate Churches." What God was really saying is IF we were willing to be one, we would be one (but it would require faith and major change on our part).

In the meantime, wanting to be a good Berean,[4] I went and looked for biblical evidence for this strangely wonderful doctrine. Sure enough, the whole Bible, especially, the New Testament, seems to be filled with such a notion. In fact it was Jesus who identified Himself as this "house of God" in Jacob's dream:

> *Jesus saw Nathanael coming toward Him, and said of him, "Behold, an Israelite indeed, in whom is no deceit!" Nathanael said to Him, "How do You know me?" Jesus answered and said to him, "Before Philip called you, when you were under the fig tree, I saw you." ... And He said to him, "Most assuredly, I say to you, **hereafter you shall see heaven open, and the angels of God ascending and descending upon the Son of Man.** (John 1:47, 48, 51)*

There are two things that stand out to me about His statement. First, Jesus said that *"hereafter"* Nathanael, and we, would see heaven open. In other words, we would be living under an open heaven...now and forever. So there's no more *"rend the heavens and come down"* earth-to-heaven prayers like in the Old Testament.[5]

Heaven was open with Jesus and it is open *now!* That alone messed up a lot of my theology, not to mention how I prayed!

I have lived through several versions of how we're to conduct spiritual warfare. We would have prophets come into our area and declare that "the heavens were like brass" over us. In other words, heaven was closed and we had to pray it open. I heard this declared several times. What they probably sensed was that there was a strong resistance to the things of the Spirit in our area, but now I know better about whether heaven is open or not. As my friend Andy Hayner[6] says, "Heaven is live-streaming, 24/7!" This point is critically important for us when we look at our place in Christ.

Jesus also talks about being the gate in other places, by which we would travel in and out of heaven *in Him* (parentheses mine):

> **I am the gate...They** (and us!) **will come in and go out,** *and find pasture. (John 10:9)*

As amazing as all this is about Jesus, it doesn't end with seeing Jesus in an open heaven, for we are His body on the earth:

> *And He put all things under His feet, and gave Him to be head over all things* **to the church, which is His body, the fullness of Him who fills all in all.** *(Eph. 1:22-23)*

Let's think this through for a moment. If Jesus is the ladder between heaven and earth where all this angelic activity is going on, and if we are now His body on the earth, *the fullness of Him who fills all in all,* then we can only come to one absolutely stunning conclusion. *We are also this conduit from heaven to earth.*

> *"Heaven is live-streaming, 24/7!"*
> *Andy Hayner*

With this understanding, let's deal more directly with some of our favorite evangelical sacred cows about heaven and the world we live in.

THIS WORLD IS NOT MY HOME?

"This world is not my home." We like to put it on plaques, write about it, sing songs about it, and a hearty "amen!" is elicited whenever these sentiments are shared. As our beloved Billy Graham would say, *"Heaven is my home. I'm just travelling through this world."* We can't wait to leave it all and be with Jesus. It's seen like some rite of passage into our maturity in Christ. We're finally *"taking up our cross."* It becomes

an indicator of a heart that finally longs to leave this world behind.

I get all that, but *why not just be home with Him now?* And with all due respect to Billy Graham (and he deserves a lot), what *should* it mean when we say, *"My home is in heaven"*?

Aren't we home with Him now? Actually…at home *in* Him now?

I certainly understand the sentiment. We want to leave this "wicked old world" and go to heaven where there is no pain and sorrow. If you're a believer and you were to die today, you would certainly go to heaven. But my questions is this: *Is dying, or flying, when you finally "go home?"*

I admit I'm going to get a bit iconoclastic here, but this doctrinal "emperor" just doesn't have any clothes. This view of heaven comes from a biblical paradigm that lacks understanding about who we are and where we are in Christ. It comes from people who only have a "theoretical" view of being in Christ, for it makes no sense any other way.

IS HEAVEN MY DESTINATION OR ORIENTATION?

Again, if you died today, you would be in a place called heaven, but this is only because your physical body can't go there. As I already pointed out from Scripture, your spirit resides in heaven now, in Christ.

We are "spiritual beings,"[7] which means our life has a heaven-born source. While it's true that our citizenship is in heaven, not earth, we are living *from* heaven now; we have *already come* to the heavenly Jerusalem, Mount Zion…now. The Kingdom of heaven is *within you* now.

Notice the tenses of the following verse:

> But you **have come** to Mount Zion, to the city of the living God, **the heavenly Jerusalem.** You **have come** to thousands upon thousands of angels in joyful assembly. (Heb. 12:22 NIV)

Notice that it does not say we will come to Mt. Zion when we die. We *have* come. Paul clearly shows that our new orientation is from there, living from heaven to earth, not the other way around:

> *For our citizenship is in heaven, **from** which we also eagerly wait for the Savior, the Lord Jesus Christ. (Phil. 3:20)*

Your citizenship is in heaven FROM which you eagerly wait....You are God's house, His building, His Temple.[8] Jesus is currently at the right hand of the Father in heavenly places and YOU are currently IN Him.[9] Therefore, you're actually home in heaven with Jesus now.

The problem is not with this world, it's with our spiritual perception.

> *Your citizenship is in heaven FROM which you eagerly wait...*

WHICH "WORLD" ARE WE TALKING ABOUT?

Another issue here is in the terminology. I was reading an excellent blog post by Frank Viola titled, "Rethinking the Second Coming of Christ" and I think he can help us clarify what the Bible means by "world." Viola says the following:

> Some have mistakenly embraced the notion that God hates this dirty little planet and has promised to rescue His people out of it before He trashes it. But Scripture teaches no such thing. Indeed, Scripture repeatedly warns that "the world" is evil. But the Greek words translated "world" in these passages do not refer to the earth, but to the world system (*kosmos*) or the present age (*aion*) that is marked by the corruptions of sin. [10]

We've already seen that "world" (*kosmos*) can mean inhabitants of the earth in chapter five (Love Shift), and that they are the objects of God's affections.[11] But in this context, it means world "system."

God seems to think that the physical earth belongs to Him, and He's given it to us.[12] God has never given the earth to the devil, so how could the earth itself be wicked. Of course, Satan is very deceptive and can get his hands on it through human beings. But the idea of an evil physical world came from dualistic[13] Greek philosophy, not by divine revelation of Scripture.

DO YOU KNOW WHERE YOUR MANSION IS?

Another significant Heaven Shift we need to make is in our thinking about this idea of getting a mansion in glory when we die and go to heaven. Is this what Jesus was talking about in John 14?

As a young Christian, I remember hearing preachers say things like, *"It took God six days to create the world but He's taking 2,000 years to prepare this place for us. How glorious it must be!"* And we would speculate about our mansion and joke about whose would be bigger. If you're over 40 years old, there's a good chance this kind of preaching or discussion is familiar to you.

Of course, there are the beloved hymns of old about our mansion in glory like this one.

> A mansion is waiting in glory,
> My Savior has gone to prepare;
> The ransomed who shine in its beauty,
> Will dwell in that city so fair.
> Oh, home above,
> I'm going to dwell in that home;
> Oh, home of love,
> Get ready, poor sinner, and come. [14]

This sentiment about mansions comes from the King James Version of John 14:2:

> *In my Father's house are many **mansions**: if it were not so, I would have told you. I go to prepare a place for you.*

I embraced this idea of a future mansion awaiting me wholeheartedly; that is, until I actually read what Jesus was saying in context. As I already mentioned in chapter two (Father Shift), we must understand that John 13:31-17:26 is one single discourse. When you read this discourse as one message, you will soon find Jesus was telling them, and us, how to *actually* do what He did—live like He did as a son empowered by the Spirit and living in the Father's embrace.

Unfortunately, our traditional idea of "mansions in glory" comes from the translator's rendering of the Greek word *monē*. The word is only used twice in the New Testament, both times in the same passage—John 14:2, 23. It means *"a stay in any place; an abode, dwelling, home."* [15]

> *You have your mansion in glory dwelling in you right now.*

What gets lost in the translation is that the English word "mansion" means something entirely different to us. Other translations render it in a less confusing way, usually as "dwelling places" or "abodes." Here's the only other place this word is used in Scripture in John 14:23 (brackets added):

> *Jesus answered and said to him, "If anyone loves Me, he will keep My word; and My Father will love him, and We will come to him and make Our **home** [monē] with him.*

My question about this verse is this: *when* does Jesus and the Father promise to come and make their "home" with us? Is it when we die and go to heaven or when the Holy Spirit is given?

If this is what Jesus is talking about here, why do we make up stories about getting mansions in glory when we die and go to heaven? The context of this "home," based on John 14:23, is clearly about *when the Helper—the Holy Spirit—comes.* It's when Jesus sends the promise of the Father to us.[16] Why, then, wouldn't this "mansion" be available to us now in the Spirit? Jesus seemed to think it would be.

In John 14:16, Jesus says the Holy Spirit will come and *"abide with you forever."* Later, in John chapter 15, Jesus tells us *how* to "abide" in this "abode." The Greek word for "abide" is *menō*. That is, to *stay* or *continue* where Christ placed us via the indwelling Holy Spirit.

Furthermore, in John 14, Jesus tells us directly that He is *"coming to us"* to make His home in us with the "coming" of the Holy Spirit.[17] There is no eschatological reference here. All references pertain to the coming of the Holy Spirit to live in us.

Here's another problem with this popular notion of mansions. If what Jesus is saying in these passages about the Holy Spirit being given to us is true, and it is, and if that's supposed to mean that we have to wait to die to get our "mansion in glory," then we cannot possibly abide in Christ now. That would be impossible since our "mansion" is up in heaven, only available to us when we die. Do you see this? It would also mean that He and the Father would not come and make their home in us until we die, which clearly contradicts what's being said here.

Again, we need to look at this whole passage in context. The abiding we are to be doing in this "dwelling place," that Jesus is talking about in John 14:2, is when the Holy Spirit is given. And we know that the Holy Spirit was given to the Church at Pentecost.[18]

We must shed this orphan mindset of getting mansions when we die and go to heaven and start living from heaven now, as sons and daughters, in the dwelling place Jesus prepared for us in the Spirit. You have your mansion in glory *dwelling in you* right now.

YOU'RE HEAVEN'S AMBASSADOR TO THE EARTH

If you were an ambassador representing your country in a foreign nation, you would represent your country wherever you go in that nation. Furthermore, your embassy building would be considered your nation's sovereign soil. International rules do not allow representatives of the host country to enter an embassy without permission. An attack on your embassy would be considered an attack on your country.

The same holds true with your heavenly citizenship!

An attack on you from the kingdom of darkness is considered a direct attack against Jesus and His kingdom.

This is what Jesus told Saul on the road to Damascus. He asked Saul, *"Why are you persecuting Me?"*[19] Saul, the religious terrorist, was dragging Christians out of their homes and putting them into bondage to face punishment in Jerusalem. Stephen was stoned to death in Saul's presence.[20] Think about this for a moment. Jesus considered all of this as the same thing as persecuting Him personally. Later, after his conversion, Paul gives us a great picture of this reality by telling us that we are ambassadors for Christ.[21] Here's my point. Wherever *you* go, heaven goes.

Not only do you and I represent Christ' kingdom on earth, but the King Himself lives in us and we live in Him! Wherever we lay our head down at night is heaven's home. God seems to think that people are going to meet Jesus in this world through you and me. When you speak, God wants to speak through you. This is why we need our minds renewed so that our words express our Father's heart.

> *Here's my point.*
> *Wherever you go,*
> *heaven goes.*

Therefore, like the religious orphan notion of waiting until we die to get our mansion in glory, we must also get rid of this fallacy that we're not home yet. Heaven is living in us; and wherever we live is heaven's "soil."

This is the Heaven Shift we need to make, to see ourselves living from heaven to earth instead of from earth to heaven.

YOU ARE HEAVEN TOUCHING EARTH!

Did you ever think that *you* are heaven touching earth? Jesus and Paul seemed to think so. Did you know that one of the last things that Isaiah prophesied was about you?

Here's what He said:

> *Heaven is My throne, and earth is My footstool. Where is the house that you will build Me? And where is the place of My rest? (Isa. 66:1)*

We need to answer this question. Where is the house that God built? Where is the place of His rest? Let's do the math. You're seated with Christ, and He's seated at the right hand of the Father in heaven on His throne. His footstool is on the earth and your physical body is now living on the earth. Therefore, you are, *right now*, where God's throne and His footstool connect between heaven and earth. Beloved, YOU are God's house[22]—His place of His rest!

Under the Old Covenant, the one thing David wanted to do was dwell in God's house;[23] under the New Covenant, the one thing God wants to do is dwell in you!

And this is true, whether you realize it or not, feel worthy or not. You are God's house—here He rests–24/7. So you might as well learn to rest in Him. Now, let's take it a step further...

Beloved, YOU are God's house —His place of His rest!

YOU are where heaven touches earth!

That means wherever you walk, heaven touches earth. As Jesus told Nathanael, angels are ascending and descending on the Son of Man, and you have been placed inside the Son of Man! Do you know this about yourself?

You are God's walking, talking, living, breathing place of rest.

God gave us His Spirit, not so that we would live like orphans waiting to go home when we die but so that we would live in this way: *as Jesus is, so are we in this world.*[24]

So we would live like Jesus lived—from heaven to earth. Notice what Jesus said to religious Nicodemus:

> No one has ascended to heaven but **He who came down from heaven**, that is, the Son of Man **who is in heaven.** (John 3:13) [25]

Imagine poor ol' Nick trying to make sense of this statement.

"So...Jesus, are you saying you are in heaven right now?"

Yes, Nick.

"But aren't you here with me right now on the earth?"

Again, yes...

"Oy veh!"

What Jesus was telling Nicodemus was that He was *both* in heaven and on the earth at the same time. Good for Jesus. But that's not the whole story. While this multi-dimensional quantum space trip is cool about Jesus, did you know that it's *also true about you*? Look at what Paul tells us:

> And God raised us up **with Christ** and seated us **with him in the heavenly realms** in Christ Jesus. (Eph. 2:6 NIV)

This is who you are. A heavenly being living *from* heaven to earth. You are living in two realms at the same time...just like Jesus did when He walked the earth.

Why is this important? *Because this is the Christian life—our life is Christ's life.* Because this orphan-hearted world needs to know it's not homeless or separated anymore. They have not been abandoned by God. He has come to meet them and live among them—even within them.

This is who you are. A heavenly being living from heaven to earth.

Our heavenly Father did this first through Jesus. Now, He's living among them *through you!* They need to know this Good News so that they can experience a life lived in the Father's embrace like we do.

Of course, we need to know and experience this for ourselves first. But whether you know it or not, you're God's instrument to bring the orphans home to their Father.

ULTIMATELY, HEAVEN IS COMING HERE

The picture of an invisible heaven with cherub babies with wings playing harps on clouds is not what's in view. Heaven is coming to earth! We're to bring it now in the spiritual realm wherever we go, and Jesus will bring it in fullness with His Second Coming.[26]

Imagine a totally visible, open heaven in its full glory and splendor manifested on the redeemed earth—us eating, drinking, and having fellowship...together...forever...with bodies like Jesus' resurrected body.[27]

So you might as well get used to the earth being your home now.

Beloved of God, let's not abdicate our role as co-heirs with Christ in our Father's Kingdom like the orphan-hearted elder brother who abdicated his role as a son in his father's kingdom. All that the Father has is yours![28] Right now!

Do you see now how much of a waste of time it is to be waiting to vacate a place we've been told to care for and rule? I suggest that instead of wishing we could leave this planet, let's love the people in this "world" like Jesus did and show them the way home to our Father's house. After all, everyone is longing to have a home with Him. It's hard-wired in their DNA. They just might not know it yet.

A FRESH SOUND FROM HEAVEN

I believe that we're living in a time when heaven is releasing a fresh echoing sound, like a sonar beacon. And God is asking, who will respond? Before I go further, a little biblical background.

In the familiar God encounter in Acts 2:2, we find an interesting word. The word "sound" here is the Greek word *ēchos*, where we also get the English word, echo. It's only used three times in the New Testament.[29]

By contrast, the Greek word for the normal way we think of

"sound" is *phōnē*, which is where we get the English word phone or phonograph. This word is used 139 times in the New Testament. In light of this, the Wuest translation renders Acts 2:2 more precisely:

> *And suddenly there came an **echoing sound** out of heaven*
> *as of a wind borne along violently.* [30]

This echoing sound from heaven was the fulfillment of the promise of the Father, the birth of the true "House of God" on the earth. Jesus was the prototype–the "first born" of this new creation, which was unprecedented. Before this time, the world was orphaned, without God as their Father. Their hearts were such that they could only relate to Him as a distant and separate God.

Those 120 on the Day of Pentecost were waiting with open hearts, full of anticipation. They heard the sound when it came and their spirits echoed back. The world has never been the same since.

One other use of *echos* is in Hebrews 12:19. This talks about another particular group of people's reaction to the sound of Heaven on Mt. Sinai (brackets added):

> *and the **sound** [echos] of a trumpet and the voice of words,*
> *so that those who heard it begged that the word should not*
> *be spoken to them anymore. (Heb. 12:19)*

The people who heard this echoing sound refused to respond..."*those who heard it begged that the word should not be spoken to them anymore.*" And because they refused, they were left as religious orphans, having to relate to God by the rules and ritual of the Law. They traded intimacy and freedom for performance and sin management under the Law.

So which is your response to the echoing sound of Heaven?

We have two groups of people before us. Both groups represent the people of God—the Hebrews 12:19 generation and the Acts 2:2 generation.

The first group responded in fear and died in the wilderness without ever entering their inheritance rest.[31] The second group responded positively to the resounding love of God and they changed their world.

The first group missed their inheritance, not because there was no sound to respond to, but because of their unbelief. They were unbelieving believers. Their hearts were still tuned to the kingdom of Egypt instead of the Kingdom of God. They were God's free people, yet they lived and thought like slaves instead of sons and daughters.

And since both Acts 2:2 and the whole book of Hebrews are directed to New Covenant believers, the application is for us. So which is your response to this reverberating sound from Heaven? Love or fear?

Are you keeping God at a distance, satisfied with the latest version of Christian programs and packaging? Like Israel wanted with Moses at Mt. Sinai, do you want your pastor, teacher, prophet, ministry leader...to hear from God for you? Not that they can't help equip you, they should. But they should not be your connection to God's echoing voice.

So which is your response to the echoing sound of Heaven? Love or fear?

Are you walking in the freedom of the Spirit to the sound of Heaven...or under the weight of rules, control, and religious ritual?

Beloved, you *have come* to Mount Zion and to the city of the living God, the heavenly Jerusalem, to an innumerable company of angels, to the general assembly and church of the firstborn who are registered in heaven." You *are* seated in heavenly places right now. You aren't supposed to be waiting for anything.

The sound of heaven is echoing again. Are you listening?

The Kingdom is advancing. Are you advancing with it? Or are you waiting for the Kingdom to come when you die or when Jesus returns?

Today is the day...not tomorrow, or in the "sweet-by-and-by."

As the writer of Hebrews says, *"Today, if you hear His voice, do not harden your hearts."*[32]

Let's not be like the religious people in Jesus' day, where He had to tell them that Heaven *"played the flute for them but they did not dance."*[33] The Kingdom had come to them but they refused to see it. They refused to dance to the waltz of heaven.

There is a fresh sound from heaven echoing through the valleys and mountains. Can you hear it?

Heaven is waiting for your response.

CHAPTER NINE ENDNOTES

---

[1] Ecclesiastes 5:2

[2] See Mark 1:15

[3] Bill Johnson, *When Heaven Invades Earth*, Destiny Image (2003), 197-199

[4] See Acts 17:10-11

[5] Isaiah 64:1

[6] Andy Hayner, Full Speed Impact Ministries.

[7] See 1 Cor.15:46-49

[8] See Hebrews 3:6; 1 Corinthians 3:9, 16; 6:19; Ephesians 2:21

[9] See Ephesians 1:20; 2:6; Colossians 1:27

[10] Frank Viola, blog post, "Rethinking the Second Coming of Christ." Retrieved at http://frankviola.org/2013/07/01/secondcoming/

[11] See John 3:16

[12] See Psalm 24:1; 115:16

[13] Dualism, in theology, is the belief that the physical world is created through evil, existing separately from a moral God. It finds its source in Eastern religions and Greek philosophy, not in Scripture.

[14] From the hymn "A Mansion in Glory" by Daniel S. Warner (1911)

[15] *Mounce Concise Greek-English Dictionary of the New Testament* edited by William D. Mounce (2001)

[16] John 14:16-17, 26

[17] Jesus talks about "coming again" here in John 14:3, 18, 23, 28

[18] See Acts 2:1-39

[19] See Acts 9:4

[20] See Acts 7:58

[21] See 2 Corinthians 5:20

[22] See 1 Corinthians 3:16; 6:19; Hebrews 3:6

[23] See Psalm 27:4

[24] See 1 John 4:17b

[25] Some modern translations omit this last phrase, but modern scholarship is now seeing this phrase was actually in the earliest manuscripts. I discuss this in greater depth on my blog at

http://wp.me/p3I7Ty-2Xz

[26] See Revelation 21:1-5

[27] See Luke 24:39-43; Philippians 3:21.

[28] See Luke 15:31; 12:32

[29] See Luke 4:37; Acts 2:2; Hebrews 12:19

[30] Kenneth S. Wuest, *The New Testament: An Expanded Translation*, Wm. B. Eerdmans, (1961), 273. Used by permission. All rights reserved.

[31] See Hebrews 4:2-5

[32] Hebrews 4:7

[33] See Matthew 11:17

CHAPTER TEN

RELATION SHIFT

I in them, and You in Me; that they may be made perfect in
one, and that the world may know that You have sent Me,
and have loved them as You have loved Me.

- John 17:23

There is only one body of Christ. There never has been or ever will be more than one body. There are no denominations in Christ.

This point was made vividly clear to me through an encounter I had as a young believer. It was in 1982, and I was still very new to dreams and visions and the supernatural in general. I was driving home from work and all of a sudden I got a vision that was so strong that I had to pull the car over. It was so profound that I just shook and cried. There's no way to adequately describe what I saw and I certainly had no prior knowledge of such a thing.

Basically, I was suspended in heaven with lots of other people. I realized immediately that I was as intimately connected to them as I was to God, and my love for them was overwhelming. We seemed to be soaring and spinning together in what I would now call the Divine Dance (I didn't have terminology for it back then). One thing that was very clear to me was that there were no Catholics, Orthodox, Protestants, Evangelicals, Fundamentalists, Pentecostals, Charismatics, or any other version of Christianity. There was just love for one another in perfect union with the Father, Son, and Spirit.

SO WHAT UNITES US...THE BIBLE?

I tend to cringe whenever I hear people identify themselves as a "Bible-believing" Christian, or that they go to a "Bible-believing church."

I want to ask, just what exactly does *that* mean to you?

Now, before you start picking up stones, let me say that I believe that the Bible is 100% inspired, God breathed, and infallible...in the original language and original writings. Of course, there are some human derivations in the manuscript copies that we have available to us and in our English translations. But I really don't sweat those things.

Since Luther's declaration of Sola Scriptura there have been over 33,000 denominations and counting!

The real rub comes in our particular *interpretation* of what we believe the Bible is saying. As we already looked at earlier, everyone has an interpretative lens by which they view Scripture. And all our hermeneutical and exegetical tools only mitigate this bias in a minor way. Just pick up a few (hundred) commentaries from scholars and you'll soon find out!

It's noteworthy that there was only one denomination for the first 1,000 years of the Church until the "Great Schism" in 1054 AD, which is when the Eastern Orthodox Church broke away from the Western Roman Catholic Church. Then there were two. It was like that for about 463 years until Luther's Protestant Reformation in 1517. Since Luther's declaration of *Sola Scriptura*[1] there have been over 33,000 denominations and counting!

This makes me wonder. If the Pharisees were called Pharisees because they were separatists, what does that make us?

These splits are usually over doctrinal differences between "Bible-believing" Christians, so it's pointless to say that you're more correct because you are Bible believing, when most everyone can say that. It's not the Bible that folks are disbelieving, it's their interpretation of it.

DO WE NEED TO MAKE EVERYONE US?

Thinking that people are wrong because they disagree with your view is a sign a relational immaturity.

Here's a test. Are all your arguments with others to prove you are right? Do you think the world should revolve around your understanding of things? How's that working for you? In your relationships? In your marriage?

Trying to relate to one another on the basis of "being right" is just an ego trip train wreck waiting to happen. Has any healthy love relationship ever been forged on the foundation of "being right?" I'm not suggesting there is no objective truth or right and wrong. I'm saying that *our understanding* of the objective truth is usually subjective. As Oswald Chambers wisely observed:

> It takes God a long time to get us to stop thinking that
> unless everyone sees things exactly as we do, they must
> be wrong. That is never God's view. [2]

Humility and staying teachable, along with realizing that we all only see in part[3] and that there will always be more than one way to look at things until Jesus returns, are some of the hallmarks of spiritual maturity.

What if, in all our relationships with one another, we sought to understand the other person instead of trying to prove that we're right and "they" are wrong?

While our intellectual wrangling tends to shrink our hearts and further divide us, love edifies and brings us together.[4] Being gracious and ready to hear would be better, don't you think?

By the way, you can disagree with me if you want. We can still love each other.

Unfortunately, religious orphans don't relate this way. They live as though separated from God, so they divide and separate themselves from Christians who don't agree with them.

This propensity to separate and divide is based on fear of being wrong, fear of false doctrine, even fear of being rejected by God. Because of fear, they must dismiss or even demonize anyone who interprets Scripture differently than they do in order to feel safe. After all, we must protect ourselves from being wrong.

Accusations like "heretic," "false prophet," and "false teacher" are thrown around with impunity rather than trying to understand someone who may have a different perspective. This divisiveness has been going on since the beginning—the former move of God "defending the Bible" and persecuting the current move of God's understanding of the Bible.

If things don't change, we can expect that the current move of God will be the persecutors of the next move of God. And on it goes. But does it need to be like this?

Think about this for a moment. As spiritual fathers and mothers in our generation, wouldn't we want our "ceiling" of Kingdom understanding to be the next generation's "floor?"

Are we going to let our level of understanding become dogma so that the body of Christ becomes afflicted with arrested development at our point of understanding? Are we so arrogant that we think we've arrived and know all things? That, my beloved friend, is dysfunctional thinking, not spiritual wisdom.

The Kingdom of God should *always* be advancing,[5] and heaven help us if we are the ones impeding its progress. While the word of God never changes, our understanding *should* improve. That means that we may not understand what He's doing at first.

DIVERSITY, NOT DIVISIVENESS

I believe that God loves diversity, but He hates divisiveness. Here's what Paul says:

> *Just as a body, though one, has many parts, but all its many parts form one body, so it is with Christ. For we were* ***all baptized by one Spirit so as to form one body—*** *whether Jews or Gentiles, slave or free—and we were all given the* ***one Spirit*** *to drink. Even so the body is* ***not made up of one part but of many.*** *(1 Cor. 12:12-14 NIV)*

We see that while we're united by the Spirit as one body on the earth, we can express Him in many different styles and forms.

This means that we don't have to do things the same way or see things the same way, in order to be in unity.

On the other hand, Paul tells us that divisiveness proves that we're not spiritually mature. When we separate ourselves from other believers it proves we're actually worldly and acting like infants in Christ (brackets added for emphasis):

> *Brothers and sisters,* ***I could not address you as people who live by the Spirit but as people who are still worldly—mere infants in Christ.*** *I gave you milk, not solid food, for you were not yet ready for it. Indeed, you are still not ready. You are still worldly. For* ***since there is jealousy and quarreling among you,*** *are you not worldly? Are you not acting like mere humans?* ***For when one says, "I follow Paul,"*** *[insert "Catholic"]* ***and another, "I follow Apollos,"*** *[insert "Protestant"] are you not* ***mere human beings?*** *(1 Cor. 3:1-4 NIV)*

While sound doctrine is important, as long as we insist on relating to one another based on lock-step doctrinal agreement, we will stay immature and divisive. If it's based on who we are in Christ, we will be united in the Spirit.

So, beloved Catholics, Eastern Orthodox, and all you 33,000-plus variations of Protestants, isn't it time we grew up and became spiritual?

Again, there are no Catholics, Orthodox, or Protestants—Evangelicals, Fundamentalists, Pentecostals, Charismatics, or any other schisms–in heaven. There are only sons and daughters of our Father in heaven. While there's nothing wrong with being Catholic or Protestant or with denominations in general, denominational*ism* is not the heart of sonship. Shouldn't we stop acting like orphans and actually celebrate our multifariousness?

THE UNITY OF THE FAITH IS THE GOAL

Paul seemed to think that the five-fold equipping gifts are to help us come into the unity of the faith:

> ***till*** *we all come to **the unity of the faith** and of the knowledge of the Son of God, **to a perfect man**, to the measure of the stature of the fullness of Christ. (Eph. 4:13)*

I don't want to get too theologically deep, but there's a "till" here, which usually means that something is in effect until whatever it says is accomplished. This brings up an obvious question. Have we come to the unity of the faith in the body of Christ? Have we arrived, so now Jesus can come back? Do we think *like* Jesus, having *His* knowledge? Has the body of Christ demonstrated the fullness of Christ and perfect love for one another on the earth? Have we even been about accomplishing this task?

Can we be honest and just say…no.

Okay, I see that suspicious look. I'm not talking about having a huge global ecumenical conference, holding hands, and singing, "Kumbaya." And I don't think that's what Paul had in mind either.

It also certainly doesn't mean we're going to eventually agree on everything or that we even have to. I'm not talking about the spirit of unity here, I'm talking about the "unity of the Spirit."[6] There is a vast difference between the two.

We're the body of Christ, connected to the Head, not our by-laws. We're members in relationship, not scholarship. It's not so much about what you know but *who* you know that matters—Jesus. Truth is found in a Person, not a particular interpretation of the Bible. Didn't we get the memo Jesus gave the Pharisees about this?[7]

How, then, does this unity of the faith get accomplished? As long as we treat truth as our interpretation of Scripture instead of as a Person, we won't get very far, but herein lies the key.

I believe that key is found in Jesus' final prayer:

> *I do not pray for these alone, but also for those who will believe in Me through their word;* **that they all may be one, as You, Father, are in Me, and I in You;** *that they also may be one in Us, that the world may believe that You sent Me. And the glory which You gave Me I have given them, that they may be one just as We are one:* **I in them, and You in Me; that they may be made perfect in one,** *and that the world may know that You have sent Me, and have loved them as You have loved Me. (John 17:20-23)*

Ah! There it is. Did you catch it? *"That* **they may be one in Us**...*I in them, and You in Me; that they may be perfect in one...."*

That's it!

The secret to unity is to live in the reality of our "common-unity" with Jesus and the Father. When we see ourselves in union with the Father in Christ, we will see ourselves in union with one another.

We've already seen that this was the whole point of Jesus' last discourse in John's gospel.[8] He became the prototype for bringing "many sons" into this glory.[9] When we live in that reality, there is real unity. This was also Paul's prayer:

> *The* **grace** *of the Lord Jesus Christ, and the* **love** *of God, and the* **communion** *of the Holy Spirit be with you all. Amen. (2 Cor. 13:14)*

What do we find in this *common-union* through the Holy Spirit? We find the *grace* of the Lord Jesus Christ and the *love* of the Father. My friend, Randy Dean[10] calls it the "Supernatural Society!"

I'm convinced that true Christian unity *only* comes when we finally learn how to live in this Supernatural Society. This was Jesus' prayer, that we would see ourselves in this same union that He has with the Father when we received the Holy Spirit:

> At that day **you will know** that I am in My Father, and you in Me, and I in you. *(John 14:20)*

Beloved of God, this is the eternal Divine Dance that Grace and Love has invited you into…today, tomorrow, and forever!

When we don't "know" this, we continue to live outside of this Divine embrace, earthbound and separated in our minds. This is a remarkable thing in view of what's been offered to us.

The secret to unity is to live in the reality of our "common-unity" with Jesus and the Father.

But when we finally find each other in the Person of Jesus Christ, fully embraced and fully affirmed as sons and daughters in the Father's love, the outcome is *always* unity.

Our orphan fear is displaced by the Father's perfect love. And to the degree that we live in this reality, we will have the unity of the faith. I think that's what Paul was getting at in Ephesians 4:13. When the world around us sees this unity based in the Father's love, they will finally see that we are His followers because we will actually be expressing His love for one another.

ALL YOU NEED IS LOVE!

I've already talked about how God can be known in chapter three (Theology Shift). But how can we *prove* to the world that we know Him? Is it by our profession of faith? Our knowledge of Scripture? Our worship of Jesus? Our good works? Our spiritual gifts? Actually, it's none of those things. Does that surprise you?

There's lots of things we seem to think are important in the Christian faith, and we spend a lot of time and money trying to attain them. But have we done the only thing that shows we actually know God?

Have we learned to be loved and to love?

Yes, you read it right. This love is the only thing that proves we know God. John tells us this in several places in his writings. Here are a couple of examples:

> *Beloved, let us love one another, for love is of God; and* **everyone who loves is born of God and knows God.** *He who does not love does not know God, for God is love. (1 John 4:7-8)*

> **We know** *that we have passed from death to life,* **because we love the brethren.** *He who does not love his brother abides in death. (1 John 3:14)*

These passages show us that if we don't love our brethren, we prove that we don't know God. Does that mean we're not saved? I don't think so. We're saved by grace through faith alone. It's just that we have proven we don't know the God who saved us.

Whenever I teach about love, I usually get the affirming nod, but I can tell there are people waiting for me to go on to the "deeper things of God."

"Yeah, yeah, right...I get that. God is love, but..."

Actually, there is no "God is love, but...," theologically speaking. There is nothing deeper about God than love, nor is there anything about Him outside of His love. To know God is to know Love. There's nothing more to learn than to be loved by God and to love...*really.*

Faith and hope are great, but love never fails and always abides, right?[11]

Paul also said that without love, *we have nothing and are nothing*:

> *Though I speak with the tongues of men and of angels, **but have not love, I have become sounding brass or a clanging cymbal**. And though I have the gift of prophecy, and understand all mysteries and all knowledge, and though I have all faith, so that I could remove mountains, **but have not love, I am nothing**. And though I bestow all my goods to feed the poor, and though I give my body to be burned, **but have not love, it profits me nothing**. (1 Cor. 13:1-3)*

Do you think Paul actually meant *nothing*? I think so.

Are you a "Spirit-filled" Christian? Going to a vibrant Spirit-filled church? The sick are getting healed, demons cast out? That's great. Do you give thundering prophecies that always come true, with glory cloud manifestations and visions of the Third Heaven? Awesome. Do you think having and defending correct doctrine is important? Cool.

What if true spiritual maturity was totally based on our capacity to receive God's love and give it away?

Are you all about social justice? Feeding the poor and making the world a better place? That's wonderful. Are you willing to die for your faith? Admirable.

Yet, without God's love, spiritual power can blow people up. Without God's love, all our biblical knowledge and defending the "truth" becomes combative spiritual pride and petty divisiveness. Without God's love, social justice turns into nothing more than self-righteous works to make us feel significant, or worse, ease our guilt. Without God's love, our martyrdom is nothing more than religious zeal.

Without God's unfailing love, we will fail.

What if God didn't measure our spiritual maturity by our Bible knowledge, our ability to build big churches, our spiritual gifts, our willingness to serve, our zeal, our charismatic personality, or our persuasive speaking skills? Actually, all of those things are gifts from Him anyway.[12]

What if true spiritual maturity was *totally* based on our capacity to receive God's love and give it away? What if it was based on how well we've been able to enlarge our hearts—to open the spigot, if you will, in order to receive and give away a greater flow rate of this unending, bottomless ocean of God's love living inside of us right now?

Do you understand that if we don't know how to open our heart to receive His unconditional love and give it away unconditionally, we can't be trusted? Really.

What if the greatest miracle that this world will ever witness is how outrageously we love and care for one another? What if they saw us celebrating our diversity without it ever dawning on us that we need to be divisive? Jesus seemed to think that abiding in this same union of perfect love that He and Father have had from eternity would show the world God's love for them in Jesus Christ:

> As the Father loved Me, I also have loved you; **abide in My love.** (John 15:9)

Our witness to this world that tells people we are His is when they see this Divine Love overflowing our hearts and spilling out onto one another:

> **By this** all will know that you are My disciples, **if you have love for one another.** (John 13:35)

You see, the world you're trying to win to Christ doesn't care one jot and tittle about what you know about the Bible. And they certainly don't want your guilt-trip *"Come to Jesus or else"* speech!

But according to Jesus, by seeing this fellowship of love overflowing out of us from God and toward one another, they will get it, and they might just want it for themselves. This is perfect evangelism. This is so because, more than anything else, every human being on this planet longs to be unconditionally loved. They've just rarely ever seen the real thing.

Beloved, do you want to be effective for God? Learn how to love. You can only do this by first receiving His love in the Father's embrace as His fully affirmed and beloved child. And when we find His love, we will find one another in Him.

The Beatles were right. All we really do need is love.

CHAPTER TEN ENDNOTES

---

[1] *Sola Scriptura* is the belief that the truths of Christian faith and practice can and must be established from scripture alone.

[2] From Oswald Chamber, *My Utmost For His Highest*, May 6, 2014. Retrieved at http://utmost.org/liberty-and-the-standards-of-jesus/

[3] See 1 Corinthians 13:12

[4] See 1 Corinthians 8:1

[5] See Isaiah 9:7; Ephesians 4:13

[6] See Ephesians 4:3

[7] See John 5:39

[8] John 13:31-17:26. We talked about this in chapter two (Father Shift).

[9] See Hebrews 2:10

[10] Randy Dean, founder of Randy Dean Ministries

[11] See 1 Corinthians 13:13

[12] See 1 Corinthians 4:7

ABOUT THE AUTHOR

MEL WILD and his wife, Maureen, are senior pastors of Cornerstone Church in Prairie du Chien, Wisconsin. They have been involved in Christian ministry together for over 30 years. Mel is a teacher, blogger, musician, and trailblazer at heart. His passion is pursuing the Father's heart in Christ and plumbing the depths of God's grace. Mel and Maureen have been married for 35 years and have three adult children.

If you have been blessed by *Sonshift: Everything Changes in the Father's Embrace*, please consider recommending it to your network of friends and acquaintances.

For more teaching and information about having Mel come and share with your group, please contact him at:

Mel Wild
Email: mwild5658@gmail.com
Website: http://www.melwild.com
Blog: http://melwild.wordpress.com